Bread that Satisfies

Unless otherwise indicated, all Scripture quotations are taken from the *King James Version* (KJV) of the Bible.

Scripture quotations marked (NIV) are taken from the HOLY BIBLE, NEW INTERNATIONAL VERSION®. NIV®. Copyright© 1973, 1978, 1984 by International Bible Society. Used by permission of Zondervan. All rights reserved.

All rights reserved. No portion of this book may be reproduced, stored in a retrieval system, or transmitted in any form or by any means – electronic, mechanical, photocopy, recording, scanning, or otherwise – without prior written permission of the author.

Transcribed by Diane Narlock

Edited by Brad Shirley

Cover Image: Copyright © Paul Maguire www.crestock.com

Copyright © 2009 Dr. Leonard Gardner
All rights reserved.
ISBN: 1-4392-5806-6
ISBN-13: 9781439258064

Visit www.booksurge.com to order additional copies.

Bread that Satisfies

An Intense Hunger for the Person
and Presence of Jesus

Dr. Leonard Gardner

2009

Bread that Satisfies

CONTENTS

Foreword	xiii
Chapter 1—The Blessedness of Hunger	1
Chapter 2—The Love Call of the Hart	11
Chapter 3—Hopelessly In Love	21
Chapter 4—Pursuing the Resurrected Lord	31
Chapter 5—That I Might Know Him	41
Chapter 6—The Need for Daily Bread	53
Chapter 7—Returning to the House of Bread	65
Chapter 8—The Odor of the House	73
Chapter 9—Honoring His Presence	83
Chapter 10—Abandoning the Past for Jesus	93
Chapter 11—Remaining Vibrant and Whole	103
Chapter 12—Satisfying Your Hunger	117

God is speaking to His Church that the number one thing, and most important, is an "intimate relationship" with Jesus Christ. He <u>longs</u> for His kids to sit down and eat of the Living Bread and drink of the Living Water. Dr. Leonard Gardner has touched a vital chord with his book *Bread that Satisfies*. This book will help you move into God's secret place and make God more real, prayer more real, and worship more real. You will be filled to overflowing with His joy. I've known Leonard for 35 years, and I have preached in his church that he founded and pastored for over 50 years. He is a forerunner of the things God seeks for. His burden is to help you enjoy and be comforted by God's presence.

Dr. Emanuele Cannistraci, CEO and founder, Apostolic Missions International

The Hebrews called the bread that was in the tabernacle the "Bread of His Presence." The Mishnah gave clear instructions regarding the replacement of this bread in the Tabernacle. Two priests would enter the sanctuary first, carrying the fresh bread. Two other priests would remove the old bread from the table, and the four priests would replace it with fresh bread, thus assuring that fresh bread would always be present in God's holy tabernacle. This is a type of what you will find within this book. Sitting under Dr. Leonard Gardner's ministry for almost 30 years, we found that he consistently fed us fresh bread. May God grant you revelation as you read this book, and may you taste of that heavenly bread, the Bread of His Presence, the only true bread that satisfies.

Bill and Jan Fahrner, Senior Pastors, Zion Christian Church— Chatham, Ontario, Canada

One of the greatest treasures we can give our children is a rooting in relationship with the person and presence of Jesus Christ. I have been blessed beyond measure to have parents who taught me spiritual and eternal values that truly matter. My father, Dr. Leonard Gardner, is deeply anointed and gifted with divine revelation from God's Word. His excellent teachings on the person and presence of Jesus found in this book will undoubtedly bless your life and draw you closer to the Lord. These teachings are theologically accurate and excellent, but even more exciting—you will find each morsel of Bread satisfying to your spiritual life as you experience and learn from my father's close walk with God.

Dan Gardner, Worship Arts Ministry Pastor, Zion Christian Church—Troy, Michigan

While journeying in the wilderness, God fed His people with *bread* from heaven called manna. By the brook Cherith, He commanded ravens to feed *bread* to the prophet Elijah. Through the miracle working hand of Jesus, He multiplied five loaves of barley *bread* to feed five thousand men plus women and children. Many other times Scripture records that He faithfully fed the hungry, but even more importantly, that He desires to satisfy the spiritual hunger in people today. In this book, *Bread that Satisfies*, Dr. Leonard Gardner, my father, addresses the importance of hunger, the blessing of being hungry, and how the provision of the person and presence of Jesus satisfies that need. You will be blessed by this book.

Don Gardner

I consider myself to be a spiritual son of Dr. Leonard Gardner. His new book *Bread that Satisfies* is a wonderful collection of messages that should be considered spiritual food to a hungry nation. Birthed in revelation and anointing, this book challenges those whose walk has grown stale to grow spiritually, excel daily, and walk boldly for God. It should be considered a "must read" for anyone who wants more of God in this season and is willing to shut down the sound of their voice to hear His! I came away not merely convinced, but moved. I highly recommend this book to all who are hungry and are seeking faith, trust, and hope.

D.L. Harville, Pastor of New Life Ministries Worldwide—Harper Woods, Michigan

I have known Dr. Leonard Gardner for many years and see him as a spiritual father in my life. Having had the privilege to read most, if not all, of the many books he has written has been very rewarding. His ability to make a biblical truth come alive so that it produces fruit not only in you but others is profound and remarkable. You can see in his life and the word that he brings that the Bread of Heaven has been a steady diet for him. I know that this book *Bread that Satisfies* will cause you to hunger and thirst after the Lord Jesus Christ.

Dr. Eddie Mitchell, Senior Pastor, RiversEdge Church—Montgomery, Alabama
President, RiversEdge International Fellowship

We've known Dr. Leonard Gardner since 1987. We've been deeply touched through his revelatory teaching which has changed our lives dramatically. He's truly a man who lifts up Jesus, loves Him deeply and knows Him intimately – a true father in the faith. His gift of mercy and compassion displayed through humility gives us a glimpse of the character of Christ. *Be warned*—you'll not find a watered down "social" gospel or the hype of the latest fad in this book. Instead, you'll find a pastor's heart concerned for God's sheep and His church, genuinely motivated through love.

Bill and Diane Smith, Care Pastors, Zion Christian Church – Troy, Michigan

FOREWORD

As far back as I can remember, I've always loved bread. In fact, without hesitation, I still call it my favorite food.

I was born near the end of the Great Depression. As such, my family never possessed much of this world's goods, but our little home was always clean and full of love for Jesus and for each other. Our lives were rather simple and much of our food came from the skillful hands of my mother who loved to cook and bake. I still remember the mornings I would awaken to the aroma of fresh bread in the oven. I believe some of my first thoughts were "This is the day the Lord hath made..." as I hastened into the kitchen to make sure the bread didn't grow stale from neglect.

Growing up in a Christian home and an excellent full gospel church, I was taught to love Jesus and honor the Word of God. As a result, I learned that bread was a type of Jesus (John 6:48) and His Word (Matthew 6:11). God's grace was upon my life and I soon discovered that the insatiable hunger I possessed for natural bread was also being manifested as a deep and growing hunger for Jesus and His Word. Similar to my experience as a boy, I still often awaken to a sense of His presence in my room, accompanied by a fresh word of Scripture in my spirit and a new song in my heart (Isaiah 50:4-5). Desiring to cherish that aroma, I immediately pursue a time of prayer and fellowship with Him. Mornings are my special time of the day.

I am convinced that regardless of what we need or think we lack in our lives, our real need is Jesus....and the way to get Him is to get hungry. We need to seek an unhindered, uncompromised, unquenchable, unending hunger for Him and His Word. If we are ever to find satisfying fulfillment in life, a hunger for God must become the driving force of our lives (Matthew 5:6). Too many have stopped short, seeking only a series of "bless me" touches. There is so much more. Hunger is the key!

I love the words to the chorus of an old song written by Bill and Gloria Gaither. They speak the cry of my heart as I pursue His invitation to know Him more. The lyrics say,

> *"More of you, more of you.*
> *I`ve had all, but what I need is more of you.*
> *Of things I`ve had my fill, and yet I hunger still.*
> *Empty and bare, Lord hear my prayer for more of you."*

In a relatively recent article about the importance of the presence of God in our gatherings, Tommy Tenney made some powerful observations. He wrote, "In many American churches today, we have replaced the presence of God with programs, traditions, and hype. The priority of God's presence has been lost in the modern church. We are like bakeries that are open but have no bread. We have become accustomed to accepting the unfulfilling chitchat that goes on around cold ovens and empty shelves."

Recorded in Isaiah 55:2, the prophet echoes a cry from the heart of God in the words, "Why do ye spend money for that which is not bread? And your labor for that which satisfieth not? Hearken diligently unto me and eat ye that which is good, and let your soul delight itself in fatness (abundance/rich nourishment)". Many people in our world are in desperate pursuit of filling the void and emptiness in their lives while overlooking the satisfying provision that comes only from the Lord and His presence (Psalm 16:11).

This book, entitled *Bread that Satisfies*, is comprised of a collection of transcribed messages I have shared over the past several years. I pray you will find them nourishing to your soul and, as a result, experience a renewed hunger for the manifestation of the person and presence of Jesus in your life and church.

Dr. Leonard Gardner

CHAPTER I

The Blessedness of Hunger

Matthew 5:6 declares, "Blessed are they which do hunger and thirst after righteousness, for they shall be filled." We are highly favored of God when the Holy Spirit produces in us a hunger and thirst after righteousness. The result, the promise, is we shall be filled. Therefore, as the Holy Spirit works in each of our lives creating hunger and thirst after righteousness, we should identify it, embrace it, respond to it, rejoice in it, and know that we are about to come into a place of being filled like never before.

The Greek word *chortazo* is the word which is translated "filled" and it means "to be satisfied, to be complete, to be whole, or to be fulfilled." It is important that we understand this as "filled" as opposed to "empty." It has nothing to do with the quantity contained, but it has everything to do with a state of bliss, of being wholly satisfied. This is contentment such that our heart is at rest and in peace, and there is no void or emptiness in us. That is a tremendous promise given to us by God.

We can be filled with many things in the world and yet not be satisfied. Many Christians, before they were in Christ, were filled with activities, events, and pursuits, but those things in and of themselves do not satisfy. True satisfaction can only be found in Christ Jesus. He's saying to those of us that will take the time to be alone with Him that He desires to satisfy us, and He tells us how He goes about doing it. Here is the condition: "I will cause you to hunger and thirst after righteousness." In keeping with the theme of this book, we are going to concentrate our focus on hunger.

Physical Hunger

God designed a tremendous phenomenon in our physical hunger. Sometimes we take these things for granted. Hunger is so much a part of our natural lives that we may not realize the significance and importance of the mechanism which God built into us. He knew, for instance, that in order for life to be sustained, we were going to have to receive nourishment.

Hunger is a physiological sensation. The appetite center in the human body is called the appestat. It is comprised of activity in both our stomach and our brain. When we experience hunger it not only comes from our stomach, but also from our brain. They work together.

In God's physiological design of the human body, He created the duodenum, located at the bottom part of the small intestine, which sends out a signal when the body needs food. The stomach reacts and the muscles begin to cramp as the need for food is sensed by the body. However, not only is there something going on in the stomach, but there is also something happening in the brain.

The hypothalamus of the brain is comprised of bilateral nerve cells. These nerve cells are designed such that on one side, the lateral nuclei react and produce a sensation, saying, "You need to eat." On the other side, the ventromedial nuclei produce just the opposite sensation and say, "Stop eating." It's awesome the way God designed us with this on/off mechanism in our bodies.

When the duodenum and hypothalamus signal to us, we must respond and receive nourishment. The body receives nourishment and life is sustained. God has built these devices into us so that we can enjoy health, strength, and the fullness of life. Indeed, we are "fearfully and wonderfully made." (Psalm 139:14)

Spiritual Hunger

Jesus is teaching us about spiritual hunger by using the analogy of physical hunger. He is effectively saying that the Holy Spirit is charged with creating in us a spiritual hunger. The Greek word for hunger is *peinao*, and speaks of being desperate for nourishment, experiencing gnawing pains, and literally starving. It is one of the strongest words in the Greek language and it describes something that is a matter of life or death. It's not like casually saying, "It is noon so it's time to eat." Rather, it's like desperately saying, "If I don't eat something I'm going to die. I'm at the very brink of starvation. I am famished."

Most of us in America may use such phrases occasionally, but we likely don't truly understand them. Tragically though, many people around the world live daily at the brink of starvation. When they eat or drink, it is literally a life saving action. It is not just a time consuming activity or habit. It is a matter of life and death. That's the meaning of the word translated "hunger" in the Greek language. It's neither trivial nor optional; it's essential. It <u>must</u> happen or we will not live.

When we experience desperate spiritual hunger, it is because the Holy Spirit is at work in us. Deep spiritual hunger does not produce simply a casual interest in God; it produces a deep passion for God. It's the difference between saying, "Please don't tell me I have to sing that chorus again" as opposed to saying, "Jesus, I can't sing enough about you because I love you so much." It's the difference between asking, "Do I have to read my Bible every day?" as opposed to saying, "Where is my Bible? I need the Word of God to make it through today." It's not simply a daily habitual activity; it's a matter of life. Jesus is saying that the Holy Spirit creates this in us.

An Ongoing Condition, Not a One Time Experience
The very tense of this Greek verb indicates that hunger is a continuing action. It isn't just a one time experience, but rather something which will be intermittently intense throughout our entire lifetime. Likewise, the Holy Spirit will create a hunger in us such that we want more of God's presence and His Word. Jesus was literally saying, "Blessed is he that _continues_ to hunger."

Righteousness: The Object of Hunger
The object of our hunger is critically important. Some people have an ungodly appetite for ungodly things. Satan can produce an ungodly appetite, but an appetite for ungodly things can never be wholly satisfied. Some people search after things in the world, and their search becomes intensified, but they are never satisfied. If we pursue sin, we will never be satisfied. It will end in death, but it will never fulfill us because there is no fulfillment in sin. The only fulfillment is in Jesus. There is an object of the intense ongoing gnawing cry, the desperate need, that we experience within us as a result of the work of the Holy Spirit. The object is righteousness. "He that hungereth…after _righteousness_…" The Greek word translated "righteousness" is *dikaiosune*, and is defined as "the character, or the quality of being right, good, or just."

Matthew 5:20 states, "I say unto you that except your righteousness shall exceed the righteousness of the scribes and Pharisees ye shall in no case enter into the kingdom of heaven." Jesus referred to the righteousness of the scribes and Pharisees, who had established a code in an attempt to satisfy certain moral and ethical standards. In a very real sense of the word, that is a form of self-righteousness, and any group can define a code which could be considered self-righteousness. Some codes are at a higher moral and ethical level than others, but Jesus was revealing something important by referring to the scribes and Pharisees. These men were practicing the highest moral and ethical level of righteousness developed by human beings at that time. However, the highest level of human self-righteousness falls far short of the righteousness of God.

God Is Righteousness

Isaiah 64:6 declares, "We are all as an unclean thing, and our righteousness is as filthy rags. And we all do fade as a leaf; and our iniquities, like the wind, have taken us away." Our righteousness, which may be impressive in our sight, is not impressive in God's sight. There is no way that humans can produce a code of righteousness that is like the Lord's. Where then is our hope? Our hope is in seeing the righteousness of God. When Jesus speaks of righteousness, He's not speaking about an <u>action</u> of God, but rather an <u>attribute</u> of God. It isn't that God just does righteous things, which of course He does, but it is that God <u>is</u> righteousness. You cannot separate the attribute from the person. If you're going to have the righteousness of God you must take God, and if you take God then you get the righteousness of God. Righteousness is an attribute of God.

In I Corinthians 1:30, Paul said about Jesus Christ that "<u>He is made unto us</u> wisdom and <u>righteousness</u> and sanctification and redemption." The very essence of God's being is righteousness. If God is righteousness, and I seek after righteousness, then by definition I seek after God. Another interpretation of this principle could be: "They that hunger after the fullness of God, all that God is, the presence of God and the person of God….shall be filled." We have become acclimated to seeking after what God <u>does</u> rather than who God <u>is</u>. Our prayers are often, "Bless me, feed me, change me, touch me." We tend to seek after what He does, while He desires that we seek after who He is. The joy is in the fact that when we get <u>Him</u>, we get everything He does and also everything He has. You've heard it said, "Don't seek healing, but rather seek the healer." That means when we have the healer, we not only have healing, but we have health.

A Desperate Craving for God

Jesus is teaching us that the Holy Spirit will create in us a craving and desperation for God until we are dissatisfied with anything less. I believe that once we have a genuine encounter with Him, we will never be satisfied with religion again. There is something about the fullness and the presence of the Lord that is fulfilling and satisfying. We must understand this principle, because this is the difference between people that are simply involved in religious activity and those that are empowered from on high.

Where is the power of God? The power of God is in God, and when He is in us, so is His power. Jesus is communicating the importance of understanding that spiritual life, satisfaction, and fulfillment can only be experienced in His person. In the same way that we cannot sustain life in our physical bodies without an outside source of food or water, it is likewise true in a spiritual sense. Jesus said, "I am the bread of life." (John 6:35) He didn't say, "I give the bread of life," such that we would run to Him at least three or four times a week to get a loaf. That's religion. There's a higher way than running to Him and getting a loaf, and that higher way is understanding that when we receive Him, we have bread as a continual supply.

Chapter 4 of the Gospel of John speaks of a woman who went to Jacob's well every day with her bucket. That was her lifestyle. A bucket full, another bucket full, and another bucket full. The man at the Gate Beautiful (Acts 3:1-10) was asking alms everyday, day after day. He was going from basket to basket, as she was going from bucket to bucket, simply surviving. Peter said, "Such as I have, give I unto thee. In the name of Jesus Christ of Nazareth, rise and walk." The man leaped to his feet and ran into the temple glorifying God. What did he have now? He had Jesus; he didn't just have a basket full. The woman ran back into the city. What did she have now? She had Jesus; she didn't just have a bucket full. During her lifetime, there were six men who had played significant roles in her life—five husbands plus the man who was currently in her life – but none of these six men brought fulfillment to her heart. Jesus was the "seventh man," and when she met Him, everything changed. Jesus effectively said, "I'm not here to fill your bucket. I'm here to eliminate your need for a bucket and give you water whereby you will never have to run to the well again. I'm going to fulfill you, complete you, and satisfy you. I'm not just one more man; I'm the Son of God. I'm going to move into your life."

Jesus Is Everything

In a very practical sense it's not so much about us getting more of Jesus as it is about Him getting more of us. We must get the clutter out of us that hinders Him from filling and occupying us completely. He is everything. He is the fullness of God. The question is, "How much do we really want Him?" Is it a matter of survival? Have we come to the place where we can't live without Jesus? If we have, that's the result of the Holy Spirit moving in our lives. That's a hunger that is absolutely supernatural. He is the joy and the sustaining power of our lives. As the Holy Spirit increases our hunger for Him, He is ushering us into the place of increased satisfaction and wholeness.

Jesus said that we are very fortunate when we have a craving desire for Him and the fullness of His presence, because we are going to be fulfilled and satisfied. I've served the Lord for all of my knowing years, and I can honestly say I love Him more now than ever before. Some may think that after seventy years of serving God, one may become bored. I disagree. You can't get bored with Jesus. You can get bored with religion very quickly, but not with Jesus. His mercies are fresh every morning. You are highly favored when the Holy Spirit is creating a longing, a desire, and a cry in your heart for Jesus because it's prelude to an ever increasing fulfillment. It's not a case of submitting to activity, talking about Jesus, or singing about Him; it's a case of enjoying and experiencing Him more and more. This results in a lifestyle of communion and fellowship with Him. It's talking and walking with the One that is living in me and is the very essence of my life.

I once heard the story of a father who gathered his children together everyday at the dinner hour and instructed one of them to assign the seats. To another, he said, "It's your assignment to set the table." To another, "It's your assignment to bring the centerpiece." At the appointed hour they would all come and sit in their seats, with the table set but with no food on the table. The father would stand and speak to them about how wonderful steak and French fries taste. Then he would get the cookbook and read several pages from it. Then they would all stand and sing a song about ice cream and strawberries. Day after day this scenario would be repeated. One day as they finished this routine, one of the boys raised his hand and said, "Dad, this all sounds good, but I'm hungry." The rest of them turned and looked at him in horror, and said, "What a fanatic!" A few days later when they gathered together, this same son showed up late. He ran in, pulled his chair up to the table, raised his hand, and said excitedly, "Dad, I took a walk today, and at the house down the street I ate some steak, French fries, ice cream, and strawberries, and I want to tell you they are everything you said they are, and more!" Having dared to do that, he was excommunicated by the family.

Jesus is more than someone to talk about, more than someone to sing about. He's someone to enjoy. Blessed are they that hunger and thirst after righteousness for they shall be filled. Are you hungry?

CHAPTER 2

The Love Call of the Hart

There are five books located in the middle of the Old Testament that are categorized as poetic books—Job, Psalms, Proverbs, Ecclesiastes, and the Song of Solomon.

The Song of Solomon is also called The Canticles. The word "canticle" means "a chant (sung or spoken) that is set to a melody." The Song of Solomon is a book of genuine love – it is a love song. It provides us with pictures of God's love through the use of metaphors and similes. A *metaphor* is a figure of speech in which something is spoken of as if it were a different thing. For example, John the Baptist used a metaphor when he pointed to Jesus and said, "Behold the Lamb of God" (John 1:29). Obviously, Jesus was not literally a lamb. He was a man, the Son of God, but He came to function as the Lamb of God, the final and perfect sacrifice.

Another figure of speech is a *simile* which compares two unlike things which are often linked by the word "like" or "as." Similes are used in the Bible to help us see the unknown by relating it to something with which we are already familiar. An example of a simile is found in Isaiah 40:31, which states that as believers who wait upon the Lord, we can mount up with wings <u>as</u> eagles, run and not be weary, and walk and not faint. To understand what that means, we must understand the capabilities and instincts of the eagle. For example, the eagle can soar above the fiercest storms. Therefore, we can conclude that we have the God-given ability to soar above the "storms" which we face in our lives. When we understand the eagle's attributes and lifestyle, we will understand all that God wants us to be able to do as believers.

Please consider a metaphor which contains within it a very important simile. Song of Solomon 2:8-9 declares, "The voice of my beloved! Behold, he cometh leaping upon the mountains, skipping upon the hills. My beloved is like a roe or a young hart." My beloved, Jesus, "<u>like</u> a young hart; behold, he standeth behind our wall, he looketh forth at <through> the windows, shewing himself through the lattice."

Verses 10-13 state, "My beloved spake, and said unto me, Rise up, my love, my fair one, and come away. For, lo, the winter is past, the rain is over and gone; The flowers appear on the earth; the time of the singing of birds is come, and the voice of the turtle is heard in our land; The fig tree putteth forth her green figs, and the vines with the tender grape give a good smell. Arise, my love, my fair one, and come away."

Please notice that the word "beloved" is repeated in verses 8, 9, and 10. "Beloved" is a name that is often used in the Bible about our Lord, and it literally means "the lover." He is the lover of our soul. Also, please note that Scripture doesn't say "a" beloved but rather "my" beloved. The word "my" speaks of possession and indicates that there is a relationship that exists. When you can call something "yours" it means a connection has been made. Jesus is "my" Savior, not just "the" Savior. He is not just "the" Lord; He is "my" Lord. He is "my" lover, "my" beloved.

Like a Young Hart

This story begins with an acknowledged relationship between the believer and the Lord, and the Holy Spirit proceeds to paint a picture for us. Scripture says that the Lord is like a young hart who desires to reveal Himself to us. In Bible times, there were three species of deer that lived in Palestine. The most predominant species was called the red deer because its fur had a red cast. This deer stood four to five feet at its shoulders and had antlers with ten or more points. When the male reached five years of age, it was called a hart. Similarly, when the female reached the age of three years, it was called a hind.

In the Old Testament, the hart is mentioned eleven times and the hind is mentioned ten times. In Chapter 2 of the Song of Solomon, the Holy Spirit focuses on the hart to give us a picture of the love relationship that ought to exist between the Lord and the believer. He effectively says, "I want you to see me like a hart." He also tells us that this hart is standing on the other side of the wall. The wall referred to in this passage is the wall of a house as opposed to the wall of a city. He is standing on the other side of something (the wall) that is separating us from Him, but He is looking at us through the window lattice.

Arise

Lattice was a common way to cover window openings in Bible times. Openings were necessary to provide ventilation in houses, but they needed to be screened in order to keep potential intruders out. Thin strips of wood or metal were crossed diagonally over the opening to form a lattice. The "word picture" given here is of a hart, representing our Lord, standing outside our wall and looking through the lattice, watching us.

What is He doing there? What does He want? Why does He come our way and reach out to us? Why is it that He has so much interest in us? The answer is in verse 13 where He says "Arise my love, my fair one, and come away."

The word "arise" implies that we are resting on a bed and He's saying, "I want you to get up from where you are. I want you to come higher." The Word of God speaks of several kinds of beds—beds of self-centeredness, weariness, laziness, and sin, to mention a few. God is calling, "I want you to get up from where you are. Arise!" Then He says, "I want you to come away with Me. I'm going somewhere. I'm doing something. I want to include you in My plan. I want you to be part of what I have in My heart to do. I'm calling you and pleading with you. Arise and come with Me. I want more than just a legal relationship with you."

Clearly, God desires for us to know Him beyond the intellectual realm and to learn to know Him in the experiential realm. Knowing Him in the intellectual realm is good. It's good to attend classes, go to Sunday School, study and learn, but God desires more than that for us. He says, "I want to walk with you and talk with you. I want you to know Me. I want to be as real to you on Monday as I am on Sunday. I want you to know that I'm with you, walking with you all day, every day." God is calling, saying, "Come away with Me."

Walking With Him

We don't truly know anyone, even in the human realm, until we walk with them. For example, in marriage you can possess a license that declares you are legally married, yet still not know your spouse as intimately as God intended. Likewise, you can be "legally" related to God through salvation, but He wants more. He wants you to be experientially related to Him, meaning He wants you to know Him in every experience you go through in your life. He wants you to know that He's with you. You can call on Him. He cares about you. He has the answer to your question. He wants to help you in time of need. He wants you to know that you are not alone. He is not a God who is far away, intangible and impersonal. No, He's your lover and He wants to be with you. He wants to walk and talk with you.

The lyrics of the beloved hymn "In the Garden" state,

"And He walks with me and He talks with me, and He tells me I am His own.
And the joy we share as we tarry there, none other has ever known."

You can't explain or compare it. He said, "Come away with Me. I want to take you to a new place. I know we're already related but I want you to enjoy a more fulfilling lifestyle. I want you to experience intimacy." I believe each of us longs for intimacy in our relationships. We want to be assured that people whom we love are going to be there for us tomorrow; that they won't leave us even when they learn all about our idiosyncrasies, peculiarities, moods and temperament. We want intimacy.

The Love of God

God loves each of us deeply regardless of whether we feel we are lovely or loveable. He loves us even though He knows everything we've ever said or thought. He not only knows our past, but He knows our present and future. He knows what we are going to think and whether we are going to fail. He knows things about us that we haven't yet discovered. Jeremiah 17:9 declares, "The heart is deceitful above all things, and desperately wicked: who can know it?"

We can't comprehend the love of God. One songwriter said it well when he wrote; "If that isn't love then the ocean is dry. There's no stars in the sky and the sparrow can't fly. If that isn't love then heaven's a myth." Another wrote, "The love of God, how rich and pure, how measureless and strong."

The Lord says, "I want you to come away with me." In response to His call, we should be saying, "Lord, how can I know You better? How can I appreciate who You are even more? You're asking me to leave where I am, and to walk with You everyday. You're asking me to take hold of Your hand and trust You for tomorrow."

We all know that trusting God isn't as easy as it sounds. There is a story about a man that got too close to the edge of a cliff and fell. On his way down, he grabbed onto a limb that was growing out of the face of the cliff. As he desperately held onto it, he cried for help but heard no response. He looked down and saw that it was a long distance to the ground and knew he wouldn't survive if he let go of the limb. He looked up again and asked, "Is anyone up there?" A voice said, "Yes, this is God. Let go and trust Me." After a few moments, the man replied, "Is anyone else up there?"

In order for us to learn to trust God more, we must get to know Him better. The more we know Him, the more we will trust Him, because His trustworthiness becomes more and more apparent to us as we get closer to Him. He wants to reveal Himself to each of us, and one way He does that is by using similes like the hart to show us His characteristics. Because God chose to use the hart as a symbol of Himself, we can better understand Him as we understand the attributes of the hart. Let us consider several interesting characteristics of the hart which can help us to know God in a more intimate way.

He is Gentle

The hart is the most gentle and mildest animal in the entire animal kingdom. Similarly, Jesus said, "Come unto me, all ye that labour and are heavy laden, and I will give you rest. Take my yoke upon you, and learn of me; for I am meek and lowly in heart; and ye shall find rest unto your souls." (Matthew 11:28-30) You can trust Jesus because He is gentle and compassionate. You may have had some bad experiences in life. You may have put your trust in someone that failed you, hurt you, or disappointed you, but Jesus will never leave you, forsake you, or disappoint you. He wants you to experience Him every day as the One you can trust.

He is mild, meek, lowly, and gentle. He will never hurt you. I have learned by walking through some very hard places in life that I can trust the Lord. I have experienced occasions when people I trusted have failed me, but He has never failed. Jesus is trustworthy.

Living in Unity

The second important characteristic of the hart is that they lean upon one another and help one another. They do not live self-serving lives, but rather they support one another and live in unity with their kind. If, for example, they are swimming across a stream, the hart that is second will rest his head and neck upon the loins of the hart that is first. As such, he will expend minimum effort and, if the hart that is out front gets tired, they trade places. They are a source of strength to each other. When we swim across the streams of life, there are times we get weary. There is One that never slumbers and never sleeps and never grows weary, and we can find rest by leaning upon Him.

Isaiah 43:2 declares, "...when you pass through the rivers, they will not sweep over you. When you walk through the fire, you will not be burned." (NIV) Note that he didn't say if, he said when. It's not just a question of whether it will happen; it's a question of timing—when it will happen. The second word that I like in that scripture is the word "through." He said that we're not just going into those things; we're going through those things. It means we're coming out the other side — we will make it through!

Lover of Music

Thirdly, the hart, loves music — both instrumental and vocal music. Does that remind you of our Lord? He said, "Sing unto me a new song." (Psalm 149:1) Paul wrote to the Ephesians, "Speaking to yourself in psalms and hymns and spiritual songs, making melody in your heart to the Lord." (Ephesians 5:19) We should not only sing <u>about</u> the Lord, but also sing <u>unto</u> the Lord. It is good to sing about Him, but since we're related, should we not sing to Him? Sing unto Him—He loves music! God's the one that invented the language of music, and music still touches the heart of God.

The Enemy of the Hart

Finally, the hart has a natural born enemy — the serpent. After the fall of man, God cursed the serpent and said, "I will put enmity between you and the woman, and between your seed and her Seed." (Genesis 3:15) Who is her Seed? It's Jesus Christ. "There is going to be enmity between you and her Seed, but He's going to destroy you." The characteristics of the adversarial relationship that exists between the hart and the serpent illustrates some deep spiritual truths.

- <u>The hart has an instinctive ability to know where serpents are hiding</u>. For example, he can see a hole in the ground and know instinctively whether a serpent is in that hole. The Apostle Paul said something similar to the Corinthian church when he declared, "We are not ignorant of his devices." (II Corinthians 2:11)
- <u>The breath of the hart drives out the serpent</u>. When the hart knows a serpent is in a hole, he breathes down the hole

and the serpent comes slithering out, unable to tolerate the breath of the hart. The breath of God is the Holy Spirit. Colossians 2:15 speaks of Jesus when it declares, "And having spoiled principalities and powers, he made a shew of them openly, triumphing over them in it."

- <u>The hart attacks the serpent.</u> When the serpent comes out of the hole, the hart immediately attacks the serpent and devours it. He doesn't negotiate nor dialogue with the serpent as Eve did in the Garden of Eden. Ephesians 4:27 declares, "Neither give place to the devil."
- <u>The hart develops a profound thirst</u>. After he devours the serpent, he experiences an unquenchable thirst and begins to moan. The thirst doesn't subside until he gets to the water brook and drinks. One of the last things Jesus said from the cross, as He was devouring the powers of hell, darkness, and Satan himself, was "I thirst." (John 19:28)
- <u>The enmity has no end</u>. The enmity between the hart and the serpent continues even if the hart is dead. For example, if a man is out in the wilderness and needs protection, if he sleeps under the hide of a hart, serpents will never attack him. They fear the hart.
- <u>The blood of the hart is an antidote to the serpent's venom</u>. If someone is bitten by a serpent, an antidote for dealing with the poison is the blood of the hart. Spiritually speaking, we were bitten by the serpent of sin, which threatened us with spiritual death. Through the blood of Jesus Christ, we are saved and receive eternal healing from the curse of sin.

The hart is an amazing creature which reveals to us many of the attributes of God. For example, God is gentle, yet strong.

He loves worship and praise. He loves when we live in unity with each other. He is victorious over the enemy of our souls. He is hopelessly in love with each of us, and He desires that we hear "the call of the hart" and respond to His life-changing love.

CHAPTER 3

Hopelessly In Love

God is love, and He loves each of us deeply. The Song of Solomon provides some insights into the love that God has for us, and the way in which He desires us to love Him.

Song of Solomon 3:1-4 states, "By night on my bed I sought him whom my soul loveth; I sought him, but I found him not. I will rise now, and go about the city in the streets, and in the broad ways I will seek him whom my soul loveth; I sought him, but I found him not. The watchmen that go about the city found me; to whom I said, Saw ye him whom my soul loveth? It was but a little <while> that I passed from them, but I found him whom my soul loveth; I held him and would not let him go, until I had brought him into my mother's house, and into the chamber of her that conceived me."

Please note that all four of the above verses contain the phrase "He whom my soul loveth." Every time that the bride, who is a type of the church, speaks about the bridegroom, who is a type of Christ, she refers to him as "He whom my soul loveth." The word translated "soul" is the Hebrew word *naphesh*, which means "the whole me"—spirit, soul and body.

In Love

The word "loveth" is equally important here. It is the Hebrew word *ohab*, which speaks of a condition rather than an action. It doesn't just say "I love him," but rather, "I am in love

<u>with</u> him." I am not just *doing* something; I am in a condition of *being* in love. The strength of this word combined with the strength of the word *naphesh* can be translated this way in modern English: "With my whole being, spirit, soul, and body, I am hopelessly, madly, passionately in love with him." The bride is saying, "I am intoxicated with his love. I cannot escape it in the night or in the day. It is with me on Mondays as well as Sundays. It is not something I do, it's something I am. It's not something I put on, but it's a state of being, a condition. I am hopelessly, passionately, madly in love with him."

I believe there is something very important that God is trying to do in each of our lives. All that we know about love in the human sense is incomparable to the love of God. Human love is fragile, temporal, and superficial, and therefore so very different from the love of God. People carelessly use the word "love." Often, it is used to describe a relationship that exists between us and something visible or tangible. Many of us enter into relationship with God carrying this baggage with us. When we carry this interpretation of love, we see God as some kind of an object to which we affix ourselves in times of need, or as some additive to our lives. This kind of love makes us feel good and contributes to making us better people. However, I believe it is the dedicated desire of our Lord to lift us to a higher level such that we can relate to Him at the level of His love, not ours.

He'll come down to our level to save us, but He will then lift us to His level to love us. The kind of love relationship that He seeks to establish with His people is far beyond what we have known on the human level. It is something that we can only begin to understand as we experience it. Jesus said that the greatest commandment of all is to love the Lord your God with all of your heart, soul, and mind. (Matthew 22:37) That speaks of relationship. God said that loving Him is to be our top priority. He effectively said, "I want you to be madly, hopelessly, and passionately in love with Me." I am convinced that many of the problems that we experience, and many of the things that foster an attitude of criticism and cynicism, can be traced to a lack of love for the Lord. Jesus was speaking of a love relationship that cannot be expressed in words, but is so all-consuming that we want nothing in this world more than being in His presence. He effectively said, "This is what I want for you because this is the highest, most blessed, honorable, and wonderful thing that you will ever experience. I want you to be passionately in love with Me."

Passion

The word "passion" is an interesting word. We hear it used frequently in human conversation, but when God used the word "passion," He led us to the cross. Acts 1:3 declares that Jesus did many infallible proofs "after His passion." What was His passion? The passion of Jesus refers to the sufferings that He endured during the night of His betrayal, trial, and His death on the cross the following day. That is the period of time which is referred to as the passion of Jesus Christ.

When I look at the cross, I see something that is horrendous and repulsive. Our Lord was beaten, bruised, and blood-covered. Isaiah 53:2 declares that "There is no beauty that we should desire Him." I look at the scene and I think "murderers!" But He says, "I'm giving you My body." I look at the scene and say "Horrible!" He says, "This is My passion." My mind is perplexed, and then I suddenly realize that there is something far beyond what I know in the human sense as love. "For God so loved the world that He gave His only begotten son." (John 3:16) Suddenly I realize that even if I gave Him everything I am and ever hope to be, everything I have and ever hope to have, it utterly pales in comparison to what He has done for me.

We hold tightly to many things and consider them very important, but God effectively said, "I love you so much I'm going to sacrifice My son for you." That may sound harsh or inconsistent with our theology, but Isaiah 53:4 declares; "Surely he hath born our grief, and carried our sorrows: yet we did esteem him stricken, smitten of God, and afflicted." The Hebrew word which is translated "smitten" literally means "killed." Some argue about who killed Jesus, whether it was the Jews or the Romans. The truth is that Jesus gave His own life because of us. All of us are to blame because of our sin. We are the cause, but He did it as a love act. "Greater love hath no man than this, that a man lay down his life for his friends." (John 15:13)

Unconditional Love

I believe that we often search for the kind of relationship in which someone will love us unconditionally—"no matter what"—even after they discover our idiosyncrasies, moods, temperaments, peculiarities, and failures. The important thing is be secure in their love. We use the word love very carelessly and superficially. We can be married to someone for years and not really know them because the desire to retain our spouse's love causes us to withhold part of who we really are. We are concerned that if he or she really knew us, they wouldn't love us anymore. That's why many relationships never reach the point of true intimacy. We may wonder, "If I let you see into me would you still love me, or would you leave me?"

Yet God knows everything about us. We have never uttered even one word that He didn't hear. We have never done one thing that He didn't see. We have never had one thought of which He wasn't aware. He not only knows what we have done and what we are doing, but He also knows everything that we are going to think and do in the future. We can't find a place to hide from Him because He is omnipresent. In fact, He knows things about us that even we don't know about ourselves, and yet He loves us.

Please understand that He doesn't always love our thoughts, attitudes, or behavior, but He always loves <u>us</u>. He doesn't condone wrong actions, but He loves us so much that He will deal with us to achieve an intimate and transparent love relationship with us. This "God kind of love" is so incredible that it demands a response. We cannot ignore it or turn from it. We must respond to the love of God. He won't let us go. The devil may try to tell us that we've sinned too much, we've crossed the line, and we have gone too far – that we are beyond the reach of God's love. Don't believe that lie!

Responding to God's Love

Typically, we believe we must earn His love. Some people think that they can earn God's love by their church attendance or membership. No, He loves us all, and our love for Him should be the reason that we attend worship services and become active in a local church. We seem to have many things in our lives that compete for our attention and affection, resulting in the reality that we don't love Him enough. I'm speaking of the kind of love that awakens us in the middle of the night to worship Him. This kind of love fills our thoughts in the morning and causes the last words we speak at night to be directed unto Him. This is a consuming, abiding, passionate, and intoxicating kind of love. This is the love that says, "I can't live without Him, I can't make it without Him, I can't get through this day without Him. I need Him."

Once we've tasted of this kind of love, we won't be satisfied with anything less. Even five minutes in the presence of God will change us. It will alter our dreams, hopes, and ambitions. It will affect our choices. Otherwise, all we have is religion, which cannot even begin to compare with the kind of love to which I am referring. Religion is duty. Religion is adhering to a set of rules. Religion is going through empty motions. These things are not the basis for, nor the essence of, a love relationship with God. He desires to bring each of us to a place where we are so intensely in love with Him that we are unfulfilled unless we become involved with Him, His people, and His purpose. As such, we cannot help but tell others about Him.

Seeking God

The response that God is looking for from our lives, and the level to which He wants to lift us in our relationship with Him, is illustrated in the first four verses of Chapter 3 of Song of Solomon. These verses unveil the heart of the bride who has come to understand that He, the bridegroom (Christ our Lord), loves her.

Verse 1 declares, "By night on my bed I sought him whom my soul loveth; I sought him, but I found him not." The word "sought" is important. This scripture teaches that we should seek Him, even by night, in dark times and hard places in which we cannot see or know what lies ahead. Something in our spirit should be crying out, "Lord, I want more of you."

Recorded in Jeremiah 29:13, God said, "And ye shall seek me, and find me, when ye shall search for me with all your heart." The Apostle Paul wrote to the church at Philippi and effectively said, "My deep desire is to know Him." (Philippians 3:10) His readers may have been perplexed and thought, "But Paul, God has revealed so many mysteries to you and you have seen so many miracles and other wonderful things!" Nevertheless, Paul wrote, "I deeply desire to know Him even more. I want to know Him in the power of His resurrection, in the fellowship of His sufferings, being made conformable unto His death. In exchange, I'll consider all of my personal accomplishments as dung, trash, and garbage. They mean nothing compared to knowing Him."

Don't go to church to be entertained or educated. Don't go just to hear the preacher. Make God the reason, the center, the focus. He is everything. The bride said, "I'm seeking him because I can't tolerate any distance between us. I must get closer. I must know him better. I can't live if there is distance between myself and him." The thought of broken fellowship with Jesus can inspire us to confess our sin and repent when we fail. We must seek "Him whom our soul loveth."

Song of Solomon 3:2 states, "I will rise now, and go about the city in the streets, and in the broad ways I will seek him whom my soul loveth; I sought him, but I found him not." Please note that she rose from her bed. I refer to this as "divinely provoked restlessness." I believe that there are times that God divinely makes us restless. It is a love call for us to come closer. When we settle for mundane things and simply go through the motions, the bridegroom isn't pleased.

It's easy to commit ourselves to a lifestyle of comfort, ease, and carelessness. But the bride says, "I am not satisfied to live that way. I must find him!" So she gets up out of her bed, out of the place of ease and comfort. She moves beyond her normal routine and begins to earnestly seek him. She says, "I will not be satisfied until I get closer to him." She goes out into the streets and the broad places. There are many people who unwittingly, unknowingly, and unintentionally try to find God's love in the streets, which represent worldly places or "broad places." However, Jesus said, "Narrow is the way." (Matthew 7:14) Some people look for fulfillment in temporal things or in other people, but it will not be found there. Some look for it in the bottle, but it's not there. Some look for it in the needle, but it's not there. Some look for it in immoral relationships, but it's not there. And some look for it in religion, but it's not there either.

The bride has searched the streets but cannot find her lover there. Where is he? She didn't give up and go back to bed. She said, "I'm not going to quit until I find him. I've got to find him." The enemy of our soul will tempt us with offers to "go back to the streets" (to past habits, sins, or lifestyles). We must not go back! We must keep searching until we find Him!

Go Past the Watchmen

Song of Solomon 3:3 declares, "The watchmen that go about the city found me; to whom I said, Saw ye him whom my soul loveth?" The watchmen represent spiritual leaders, whose responsibility it is to point others to Jesus. Isaiah Chapter 21 speaks of spiritual leadership. Please note that spiritual leaders cannot fulfill you. He or she may disappoint you or fall short of your expectations, but never forget that your leader, at best, should be a pointer to Jesus. Have you found Jesus? How it must grieve the heart of God that thousands of people go to church, and participate in religious activities, yet never find or come to know Jesus. They are empty because they can't be satisfied without Him. We tend to elevate our leaders to role models or heroes. We exhaust our leaders because of our lack of personal intimacy with God. The most important thing that our leaders can do for us is to stir a desire in our hearts to draw closer to Jesus.

Song of Solomon 3:4 states, "It was but a little <while> that I passed from them, but I found him whom my soul loveth; I held him, and would not let him go, until I had brought him into my mother's house, and into the chamber of her that conceived me." It was but a little while after the bride passed the watchmen that she found her lover. <u>We must go past the watchmen to find Him!</u> God is a jealous God and He's madly in love with us. We hear great preaching and experience great worship in many churches. But our love and our focus must not be on the "watchmen" (pastor, worship leader, etc) — it must be on *Him*. Our worship isn't successful unless we have worshipped *Him*, loved *Him*, praised *Him*, and heard from *Him*. We should honor those He uses but never worship them. God's jealous of us. He wants our undivided, undiluted, uncompromised, and unconditional love for Him.

Can you imagine what would happen if the church of Jesus Christ was more than religion, rituals, and rules? How do we get there? Like the woman in Song of Solomon, we must get up off our beds and start seeking Him. We cannot quit until we find Him. We can't stop when we see the watchmen. God has some great watchmen, but don't worship them. Seek the one to whom they are pointing. Personally, from a pastor's perspective, there is nothing more fulfilling and satisfying than to see people passionately in love with Jesus.

Love God and Love People

We dare not think of Jesus as we would a human being. We are not to love Him like we love human beings. He is the Lord. No wonder Jesus, after saying "Love God," went on to say "Love your neighbor as yourself." He said, "Thou shalt love the Lord thy God with all thy heart, all thy soul, all thy mind, and love thy neighbor as thyself." We must not reverse the order of those two commandments, because if we aren't loving God, we can't love our neighbor in the way God desires and commands us to love them. If we love Him with all our heart, we become so full of His love that we find ourselves loving others with the love of the Lord. His love not only fills us, but overflows from our hearts such that we can't help but give it away to others.

He loves us, He knows us, He hears us, and He sees us. Not only today, but tomorrow, and its tomorrow. He desires that we have a deep and abiding genuine love for Him. There is none like Him. I pray that we become so madly in love with Him that those around us will feel His love and they will have a desire to know Him also.

CHAPTER 4

Pursuing the Resurrected Lord

John 20:1-9 states, "The first day of the week cometh Mary Magdalene early, when it was yet dark, unto the sepulchre, and seeth the stone taken away from the sepulchre. Then she runneth, and cometh to Simon Peter, and to the other disciple <John> whom Jesus loved, and saith unto them, They have taken away the Lord out of the sepulchre, and we know not where they have laid him. Peter therefore went forth, and that other disciple, and came to the sepulchre. So they ran both together; and the other disciple did outrun Peter, and came first to the sepulchre. And he <John> stooping down, and looking in, saw the linen clothes lying; yet went he not in. Then cometh Simon Peter following him, and went into the sepulchre, and seeth the linen clothes lie. And the napkin, that was about his head, not lying with the linen clothes, but wrapped together in a place by itself. Then went in also that other disciple, which came first to the sepulchre, and he saw, and believed. For as yet they knew not the scripture, that He must rise again from the dead. Then the disciples went away again unto their own home."

We call the first day of the week Sunday. It's the day that we gather together as believers to worship our Lord. I believe there are three reasons that Christians typically gather on the first day of the week. One of the reasons is right here in this passage—it was the day that Jesus arose. The second reason is that it is the day that the early church assembled together. The third reason is that it is the "firstfruits" of the week. In other words, it is the first day that He has given us, and by His grace, will give us, each week. He deserves the best and He deserves the firstfruits of all we have.

The Gospels are in Harmony

Critics of the infallibility of Scripture are quick to point to passages in the gospels that superficially appear inconsistent. Such is the case here.

In his Gospel, John wrote that Mary Magdalene came to the sepulchre. Mark and Luke both wrote that another Mary, Mary the mother of James and John, came also. A third gospel writer said there were many women that came. However, none of the other apparent inconsistencies prove John inaccurate because he didn't say only Mary Magdalene came to the sepulchre. Therefore, by implication, she's an "also." She apparently came along with other women to the sepulchre. The Gospels are in harmony with one another, and never in contradiction.

Another thing that skeptics like to criticize is the apparent contradiction concerning the women's walk to the tomb. John's Gospel states "while it was still dark" and Matthew wrote "as it began to dawn." Mark wrote "at the rising of the sun" and Luke wrote "very early in the morning." So who is right—Matthew, Mark, Luke or John? They all are correct. John was simply focusing on the night while the others were focusing on the light. John was focusing on that which was and is, while the other gospel writers were focusing on what was coming and shall be. Perspective is everything!

The Stone, the Seal, and the Guards

The women left their homes in darkness and came to the tomb at the breaking of the dawn, bringing spices which they had prepared to anoint the body of the One that they loved. They were coming to express their devotion to One who had so affected their lives that they would never be the same again. John wrote that while they were yet a distance from the sepulchre, they noticed that the very large stone, which had been rolled into place across the mouth of the tomb to seal it, was now removed. The stone had been rolled away.

When the stone was placed over the tomb, it had been sealed with the king's seal. The seal was an indication that it had been placed there under the authority of the king. The seal was not to be broken, nor the tomb tampered with in any way, under penalty of death. The scene the women beheld that morning at the tomb was a dramatic change from what they had last seen at the tomb. The stone was rolled away and the king's seal was broken. Who broke the seal? We of course know that it was the King of Kings, the only One that had authority over every other lesser king.

In addition to the stone and the seal, guards had been assigned to keep watch over the tomb so that no one would steal the body of Jesus and then claim that He had risen from the dead. The Bible says that the guards "fell as though dead" when the power of God moved the stone.

The Women's Reaction

The women arrived at the tomb to see this astonishing sight, and as they looked upon the scene they suddenly became very frightened. There was no logical explanation for what they were seeing. In their fear they came to a conclusion, surmising that someone had stolen His body. This situation was bigger then they could handle. They didn't know what to do, so they ran to tell other disciples. They effectively said, "Peter and John, we have a problem. Something has happened, something has changed. Someone has stolen the body of our Lord. We watched as He was arrested, beaten, crucified, and buried. And now, His body has vanished. We can't anoint Him with the spices we've prepared because He isn't there! Someone broke the king's seal, rolled the stone away, entered the tomb, and took Him."

John's Reaction

The Word of God tells us that Peter and John, having heard the women's report, ran immediately to the sepulchre. Apparently John was a little younger and certainly a little faster than Peter, because he arrived at the tomb first. Please note that as they approached the sepulchre, they moved beyond the point where the women had stopped. The women stopped a distance from the sepulchre and looked *upon* it. When Peter and John arrived at that place they effectively decided, "We're not going to be satisfied just to look from a distance." So, they kept running beyond that point until they arrived at the sepulchre itself. John, who arrived first, approached the sepulchre and looked *into* it. He wanted to observe what had transpired, wondering, "Is His body still there, or is it gone?" As John peered into the tomb, he saw something that the women hadn't seen because they stopped short of the open sepulchre. They stopped short of personally experiencing all that God had intended for them to experience.

When Jesus arose, He didn't roll away the stone to come out, because He could have walked directly through the stone. He rolled away the stone to let them in. Similarly, when God rent the veil from the top to the bottom to let us in, He welcomed us into the Holiest of Holies. All were welcome to enter the open tomb. There was something to be learned at the open tomb that couldn't be learned by looking from a distance. When John looked in, he saw the grave clothes lying there. He immediately knew Jesus' body couldn't have been stolen, because if it had been stolen, the grave clothes wouldn't be there. However, by implication of what John saw, Jesus' body was now free to move, liberated from every bondage and bandage that man had wrapped around Him.

Please see the spiritual significance of this. You and I, as born-again believers, are the Body of Christ, and because He lives, we live also. (John 14:19) It's His desire that we be unwrapped, unbound, liberated, and free to be a living witness of His resurrection power to the whole world. John received a glorious revelation that the women hadn't yet received (though they would later). The reason that he received that revelation is because he went beyond where they stopped. He went further in pursuit of Jesus. Please see the lesson here: *the more we pursue Him, the more we know about Him. The more we pursue Him, the greater revelation we have of Him.*

The Power of the Resurrection

The Apostle Paul expressed his personal desire in Philippians 3:10: "That I might know Him." The phrase "know Him" in the Greek language means to have an intimate relationship with Him. Many people know the facts of the resurrection, but Paul effectively was saying, "I'm not content with knowing the facts. I want to know the _power_ of the resurrection." He wrote, "Being made conformable unto his death; If by any means I might attain unto the resurrection of the dead." (Philippians 3:11)

Some believe this verse implies that Paul was stating a personal desire to possess the power to raise people from the dead. However, I see it differently because the Greek word *alpha* precedes the word resurrection, which indicates that Paul was referring to the *first* resurrection—being born again and having a true relationship with Christ. Paul was literally saying, "That I might attain unto the <u>first</u> resurrection of the dead; that I might be a part of the <u>first</u> resurrection. I am pursuing Him. I want to know Him. I will be satisfied with nothing less than to know Him more. I don't care where others stop. I'm going all the way."

Paul continues in verses 12 through 14, "Not as though I had already attained, either were already perfect: but I follow after, if that I may apprehend that for which also I am apprehended of Christ Jesus. Brethren, I count not myself to have apprehended: but this one thing I do, forgetting those things which are behind, and reaching forth unto those things which are before, I press toward the mark for the prize of the high calling of God in Christ Jesus."

Or, in other words, "I have not yet become everything that I know God desires for me to be. I have not yet attained everything that God wants me to attain, but one thing I have decided is that I am not stopping here. I'm not quitting. I am determined to *press* toward the mark for the prize of the high calling of God in Christ Jesus." The word "press" means "pursue."

Paul continues in verses 15 and 16, "Let us therefore, as many as be perfect, be thus minded: and if in any thing ye be otherwise minded, God shall reveal even this unto you. Nevertheless, whereto we have already attained, let us walk by the same rule, let us mind the same thing." When he refers to those who would be "perfect," he doesn't mean "flawless." The Greek word translated "perfect" literally means "mature; fully developed." He was effectively saying that each of us should be driven with a determination to pursue God, to know everything there is to know, and to be everything that He wants us to be.

Peter's Reaction

John got close to the tomb, saw the grave clothes, and marveled. He saw things that the women who stopped a distance from the tomb did not see. Finally, Peter arrived at the tomb. Peter may have been slow of foot but he wasn't slow of heart. Peter was an "all or nothing" type of guy. There was no "in between" with him. He passed the place where the women stopped, came to the door of the tomb, and stepped past John, entering the tomb. He was saying by his actions, "I'm not only going to <u>look</u> in, I'm actually <u>going</u> in." Please see the progression: the women *<u>looked on</u>*, John *<u>looked in</u>*, and Peter *<u>went in</u>*. John saw something that the women didn't see, and Peter saw something that John didn't see — Peter saw the napkin folded in a place all by itself. (John 20:7)

The Folded Napkin: "The Work is Finished"

The napkin was a linen cloth that was wrapped around the head of the deceased, separate from the grave clothes which bound the body. I believe the folded napkin represented two things. First, it represented the fact that the work of the head, Jesus Christ, was finished. His work was done; it was accomplished. Who folded the napkin? Jesus did. Please see this in a spiritual sense: the body (believers, the Body of Christ) has been raised with power, unwrapped from the grave clothes, and the work of the head (the spiritual Head, the Lord Jesus Christ) is finished. So we stand on, walk in, and rejoice in the truth that His work is finished. Not one more thing remains to be done by Him.

We cannot be content to stand back, compromise, or only go part way. Going part way never works. If we are going to follow Jesus, it must be all the way.

I learned that lesson as a boy. We were at a lake and my father invited me to get into his boat and go fishing. I wanted to go fishing but I wasn't confident in the ability of the boat to stay afloat. Therefore, I stepped off the dock and put one foot in the boat, leaving one foot on the dock just in case the boat sank. That turned out to be a big mistake. When I put my foot in the boat, the boat began to move but the dock did not. It wasn't long before I understood that we must either get into the boat or stay out of the boat. We cannot have one foot in and one foot out.

I believe Jesus has revelation, power, and authority available for people who will give Him their whole heart, mind, and soul, for people unwilling to compromise in any way. Peter had denied Jesus three times, but he refused to wallow in his failure, and he refused to give up. If there was more to know, he wanted to know it. If there was more to experience, he wanted to experience it. If there was more to receive, he wanted to receive it.

I believe God is looking for people like that. I believe He's looking for people that want Him more than anything in the whole world. Mark 8:38 states, "Whosoever therefore shall be ashamed of me and my words in this adulterous and sinful generation; of him also shall the Son of man be ashamed, when he cometh in the glory of his Father with the holy angels." God is effectively saying, "I'm looking for people that are not ashamed of Me, who are committed to pursue Me regardless of how many others may stop or quit along the way." This is a personal decision that each of us must make. We each decide how far we want to go, how much of Jesus we want to know. I'm always thrilled with Paul's testimony because he was a man that wrote more books of the New Testament than any other man, yet he still had a burning desire to know God better.

The Folded Napkin: "The Master Will Return"

According to Jewish tradition, the folded napkin was very significant in the relationship between a master and his servant. In that day, before the master ate a meal, the servant prepared the table. When the preparation was finished, the servant left the room and signaled to the master that all things were ready for him to eat. When the master went in to eat, it was important that the servant remained out of the room. He wasn't permitted to go in until the master was finished.

After the master had finished eating, the servant went in and cleaned up before proceeding with his other duties of the day. The master would communicate to the servant that he was finished by way of his napkin. When the master was finished eating, he wiped his hands and face, rolled up the napkin, threw it on the table, then left the room. However, if for some reason the master left the room and wasn't yet finished eating, he would take his napkin, fold it up neatly, and lay it on the table. After the master left the room, the servant went in and looked for the napkin. *If he saw that the napkin was folded neatly, he knew that the master wasn't finished and would be returning.* However, if the napkin was not neatly folded, he knew that the master was finished, so he could proceed to clean up.

I believe that Jesus folded the napkin in the tomb. It wasn't just was thrown in a pile. It was folded and lying separately from the grave clothes. Peter saw the folded napkin, which declared the Master's message: "I'm coming back!"

The day when Jesus spoke His final words to His disciples and they watched Him ascend into the clouds, they began to experience loneliness and heaviness. They must have thought, "What are we going to do without Him? He was everything to us. We left our occupations, homes, and dreams to follow Him, and now He's gone." But Peter could say, "Don't forget that *I saw the folded napkin. He's coming back!* We're not going to be left here alone and comfortless. We're not going to be left here without hope if we believe on Him. He gave us a promise. Soon, this same Jesus who left the napkin behind shall return again to receive us unto Himself."

Personally speaking, I've pursued Him sufficiently to see the folded napkin. I long to be with Him and spend eternity with Him. I have knelt at the foot of the cross. I have confessed and acknowledged that I have sinned and come short of the glory of God. I believe the blood of Jesus has remitted my sin, and because of that, I'm ready for His return.

Are you pursuing Him? Have you pursued Him to the cross? Have you received His shed blood as the only remission of your sin? Are you ready to go and be with Him when your life on earth has ended? If not, I encourage you to make that important decision today. Chapter 12 of this book will help you in that regard.

CHAPTER 5

That I Might Know Him

The twenty fourth chapter of the Gospel of Luke contains a powerful account of a post-resurrection encounter between two unnamed men and Jesus. It occurred on the evening of the same day in which Jesus arose from the grave. The two men were walking on the road to the village of Emmaus, which was located about seven or eight miles from Jerusalem. It took approximately three hours or more to walk from Jerusalem to Emmaus.

Luke 24:14 states that the two men "talked together of all these things which had happened" as they walked along the road to Emmaus. They were discussing the events surrounding the ministry and death of Jesus and were perplexed because they couldn't make sense of all that had happened.

Luke 24:15 declares, "And it came to pass, that while they communed together and reasoned, Jesus himself drew near, and went with them." Jesus always knows where we are. He knew the men needed to move beyond where they were spiritually, mentally, and emotionally. They were still lost in the confusion of Jesus' death, so He drew near and joined them. It is significant that the scripture states "their eyes were holden that they should not <u>know</u> him."

Walking with Jesus

The word "know" is a very important word. The Greek word is *epignosis,* and it means "to be fully acquainted with."

They saw Jesus physically but didn't recognize Him. They were not fully acquainted with who He was when He came to them. There was a spiritual block—their spiritual eyes were "holden." They did not understand and were very confused and dismayed, but praise God that this isn't the end of the story.

Luke continues, "And he said unto them, What manner of communications are these that ye have one to another, as ye walk and are sad? And one of them, whose name was Cleopas <which means 'the complete glory'> answering said unto him, art thou only a stranger in Jerusalem, and hast not known the things which are come to pass there in these days?" They are effectively asking Jesus, "Haven't you heard what's been going on? Aren't you aware of the recent events of our lives? Don't you know what we have been going through?" We often ask Jesus the same type of questions concerning circumstances in our own lives.

Luke continues, "And he said unto them, 'What things?'" Jesus always wants us to hear our heart. He never asks questions to be informed (because He is omniscient), but He asks questions to help us see our own heart. After He asked "What things?", the two men began to open their hearts. "And they said unto him, Concerning Jesus of Nazareth, which was a prophet mighty in deed and word before God and all the people. And how the chief priests and our rulers delivered him to be condemned to death, and have crucified him. But we trusted that it had been he which should have redeemed Israel; and beside all this, to day is the third day since these things were done. Yea, and certain women also of our company made us astonished, which were early at the sepulchre; And when they found not his body, they came, saying that they had also seen a vision of angels, which said that he was alive. And certain of them which were with us went to the sepulchre, and found it even so as the women had said; but him they saw not. Then he said unto them, O fools, and slow of heart to believe all that the prophets have spoken. Ought not Christ to have suffered these things, and to enter into his glory? And beginning at Moses and all the prophets, he expounded unto them in all the scriptures the things concerning himself. And they drew nigh unto the village, whither they went; and he made as though he would have gone further."

Abiding with Jesus

This is a very key part of the story. They arrived at their destination in Emmaus, and they were standing outside with Jesus. They were preparing to enter their home, and Jesus was standing outside, giving the appearance that He was going to continue walking. "But they constrained <compelled> him saying, Abide with us." They had an <u>experience</u> with Him on the road, and now they were compelling Him to <u>abide</u> with them "for it is toward evening; and the day is far spent, And he went in to tarry with them." Jesus always responds to everyone who will ask Him to abide with them. He went into the house with them. "And it came to pass, as he sat at meat with them, he took bread." The fact that Jesus was the one that took the bread is somewhat unusual because He was the guest. It was the host, not the guest, who was normally the one who blessed, broke, and distributed the bread. Scripture says, "He took bread, and blessed it, and brake, and gave to them." What happened? The two men had deferred to Jesus and elevated Him from being simply a guest to being the host!

Please note the order of Jesus' actions. He "….blessed it, He break it, He gave it." There is a divine order to the way God prepares us to be bread to the hungry. First He blesses us, secondly He breaks us, and thirdly He gives us. Therefore, whenever we are blessed, we should be prepared for the breaking. He does the blessing, and He also does the breaking. He doesn't break us to hurt or destroy us, but only to prepare us so that He can give us (our time, talents, and resources) to others.

Becoming Fully Acquainted With Him

Jesus blessed the bread, broke it, and gave it to the men, and their eyes were opened. Prior to that, they were unable to recognize or identify Jesus, but now "their eyes were open and they knew Him." This is the same Greek word, *epignosis*, meaning "knew Him," that we mentioned earlier. The men now recognized Him, had a revelation of Him, and were "fully acquainted" with Him. "And they said one to another, Did not our heart burn within us, while he talked with us by the way, and while he opened to us the scriptures? And they rose up the same hour, and returned to Jerusalem, and found the eleven gathered together, and them that were with them. Saying, The Lord is risen indeed, and hath appeared to Simon. And they told what things were done in the way, and how he was known of them in breaking of bread." Receiving blessings from Jesus is wonderful, but that's not where we get to know Him. That's not where we become fully acquainted with Him. That happens in the breaking and in the giving.

I believe that Jesus blessed them with His *presence* on the road so that He could give them an opportunity to know His *person*. I am firmly convinced that the reason He blesses us with His presence is not an end in itself but rather an invitation to know His person in a greater way. While they were on the road, they experienced His presence and described it as "heartburn" ("Did not our heart burn within us..."). Some may refer to it today as having goose bumps or crying or laughing. Our emotions are affected when we're in His presence. However, Jesus lingered because there was something more He wanted them to have. He wanted them to experience more than "heartburn." He wanted them to have the privilege of experiencing His Lordship in their home and in their lives.

There is a Difference

There is a difference between having a single experience with Him as opposed to having a daily walk with Him. There is a difference between knowing *about* Him, and knowing Him. There is a difference between being intellectually informed and being intimately related. The two men on the Emmaus road were intellectually informed (and their hearts "burned") as He explained the scriptures to them. However, it wasn't until they invited Him in to abide with them in their house, and they allowed Him to be the host (blessing and breaking the bread), that their eyes were opened and they realized that it was Jesus.

There is a difference between knowing the words of a chorus and being a worshipper. There is a difference between knowing Bible stories and understanding the Word of God. There is a difference between knowing where the prayer room is located and being a true intercessor. There is a difference! However, some people are content to have only an experience. We must challenge ourselves to hunger for more than the experience that produces "heartburn" in us. We must seek more than a thrill or an emotional "high." There is so much more. We are offered the ever present abiding sense of His person in our lives in which there is a continuing, perpetual intimacy; a close acquaintance with Him.

We have all heard the phrase, "You don't know a person until you live with them." It's the same in our relationship with Jesus. It is good to faithfully attend church services and hear about Him, but He wants so much more than that. He wants us to come close to Him and abide with Him so that we can know Him and become whole.

Luke 17:11-19 contains the account of Jesus healing ten lepers. He _healed_ the ten lepers (symbolically representing the born-again experience), but only one returned, fell at His feet, called Him Lord, and was made _whole_. There is a difference between being _healed_ physically and being _whole_ spiritually. Nine of the lepers received a physical blessing from Jesus but didn't experience everything that He intended for them. Only one leper was made _whole_. Lord, help us to be like that one leper, ever hungry for more of You!

As recorded in Revelation 3:20, Jesus said; "Behold, I stand at the door, and knock; if any man hear my voice, and open the door, I will come in to him, and will sup with him, and he with me." The word "sup" means "to commune." I think there is sufficient scriptural support to preach that verse evangelistically (directed to unbelievers), but primarily it is a message to believers. Jesus is effectively saying to believers, "I'm at your door. If you will let Me come in, I'll bring you into a place of communion and fellowship with Me, beyond what you have ever experienced."

Invite Him In

God desires to take us from one spiritual level to the next as He progressively reveals Himself to us. For example, no one can convince me the Lord doesn't heal because several doctors gave me up for dead when I was about three years old. After prayer, I was instantaneously and miraculously healed! No one can convince me God doesn't save, because I am saved. It's not a case of intellectual persuasion; it's a case of experiencing Him and being intimately related to Him.

After walking along the Emmaus Road with Jesus, the men invited Him to remain with them by effectively saying, "We want You to abide with us. We invite You to be our _host_, not simply our guest. We are here to learn from You. <u>You</u> take the bread, bless it, and break it. We enjoyed what we experienced on the Emmaus road when our hearts burned within us, but this is even more wonderful because our eyes were opened here."

I encourage you to call out to Him and say, "Lord, fill me with Your glory. Show me Your glory." Isaiah saw God's glory and was changed. *It changes our life when we love Him for who He is and not just for what He's done.* There is no end to the revelation of who He is. There are times when we think we've come into a deep understanding of Him, and then He draws the curtain further back and we say, "Oh my, there's even more!"

Jesus is standing outside our door, waiting and lingering. He's saying to us, "You have had some good experiences. You have had your share of 'heartburn,' but I'm waiting to give you something more. Do you want Me more than anything else in the world?" Are you willing to open the door and say to Him, "Come and abide with me? Come into my house and be the Lord of my life." If you do so, He will manifest and reveal Himself in a progressive way until you think you've experienced it all. Then He gives you even more!

We must pray that we will never lose our hunger. Jesus said, "Blessed are they that hunger." He didn't say, "Blessed are they that are filled." Filling is a consequence of being hungry. Don't seek the consequence, seek the cause. Seek the hunger, not the filling. Pray, "I'm hungry. I want to know more about You, Jesus. I want to grow closer to You. I want to be used in a greater way by You. I want You to be glorified through my life in a greater measure. Jesus, I'm hungry!"

I'm so glad that Jesus lingered at the door, waiting, when the men reached their destination after walking with Him on the Emmaus Road. He was ready to go on if they didn't want Him. He would have continued on, but He gave them an opportunity to go beyond where they were, to move beyond the intellectual place to the place of intimacy, to move beyond the "heartburn" to the revelation. Do you know Him? Do you <u>really</u> know Him? Do you want to know Him better? Do you want to know Him more? There is no limit to what He can do in your life. Open the door, invite Him in, and give Him complete control!

That I Might Know Him

Perhaps that is what was happening in the Apostle Paul's heart when he wrote to the church at Philippi, "That I might know him, and the power of his resurrection, and the fellowship of his sufferings, being made conformable unto his death; If by any means I might attain unto the resurrection of the dead." (Philippians 3:10-11) Paul wrote more books in the New Testament than anyone else, yet he still wanted to know God in a greater way. Paul wanted more than the "heartburn" experience. He wanted to know Him in a progressive way until ultimately he could see Him in all of His glory and all of His fullness.

During the latter part of Jesus' ministry, a group of Greeks came to Jerusalem to worship at the Feast of Passover. The Greeks said, "Sir, we would see Jesus." (John 12:21) The Greek word translated "see" is *eido*, but it doesn't mean "to look upon" or "to glance at." It means "to know." The men were really saying, "We want to be with Jesus, to commune, communicate, and talk with Him. We want to get to know Him."

As Jesus was praying in the Garden of Gethsemane, He said to the Father; "And this is life eternal, that they might know thee." (John 17:3) The important thing is not how many "heartburn experiences" we have had – the important thing is knowing Him! How well do we know Him? What does He really mean to us?

There are two men in the Bible that are great examples of having a deeper revelation of God. One was Isaiah the prophet. The other was John the Beloved, a disciple of Jesus.

Isaiah the Prophet

Isaiah 1:1 states, "The vision of Isaiah the son of Amoz, which he saw concerning Judah and Jerusalem." The next five chapters of the Book of Isaiah contain accounts of the utter ruin of the land and the immoral condition of the people. Isaiah had a vision in which he saw the situation of the people and the nation, but Chapter 6 is the pivotal point, as it records how Isaiah was changed forever.

Chapter 6:1 declares, "In the year that king Uzziah died I saw also the Lord sitting upon a throne, high and lifted up, and his train filled the temple. Above it stood the seraphims; each one had six wings; with twain he covered his face, and with twain he covered his feet, and with twain he did fly. And one cried unto another, and said, Holy, holy, holy, is the Lord of hosts; the whole earth is full of his glory." Isaiah effectively said, "I see it now. I see the glory of the Lord." It transformed his ministry. He had experienced a vision of the condition of the people, but now he was having a divine encounter with the glory and majesty of the Lord. Throughout the remainder of his book, Isaiah was progressively revealing the Lord. He prophesied more about the person of the Lord than perhaps any other prophet. Seven hundred fifty years before Jesus came, Isaiah saw His glory and had a revelation of Him. Isaiah described Jesus in some of the following ways.

- Isaiah 7:14: "His name is Immanuel", God with us.
- Isaiah 9:6: "His name shall be called Wonderful, Counselor, the Mighty God, the Everlasting Father, the Prince of Peace."

- Isaiah 42:1: He is called "the elect of God."
- Isaiah 51:9: He is the "arm of the Lord."
- Isaiah 53:2: He is "a root out of dry ground."
- Isaiah 53:3: He is "a man of sorrows, and acquainted with grief."
- Isaiah 55:4: He is "a witness, a leader, and a commander to the people."
- Isaiah 55:5: He is "the Holy One of Israel." Isaiah refers to Christ as "the Holy One of Israel" twenty five times in his book.

Clearly, Isaiah's life and ministry were transformed because he saw the glory of the Lord.

John the Beloved

John the Beloved also wrote of beholding God's glory. He was one of the twelve apostles. He referred to himself in his writings as "the one whom Jesus loved." John wasn't implying that Jesus didn't love the others. Rather, I believe he was saying that he embraced the reality that Jesus loved him. John heard the heartbeat of Jesus. He was the only one of the twelve that stood near Jesus as He hung on the cross. (John 19:26) He was the one to whom Jesus committed the care of his earthly mother. (John 19:27) There was something different about John. His gospel demonstrates that.

The three "synoptic gospels" (Matthew, Mark, and Luke) are similar to each other, and they speak about what Jesus *did*. John, however, wrote much about who Jesus *is*. The Gospel of John doesn't begin with an account of Jesus' earthly life, but instead John goes all the way back to the *very* beginning – before the creation of the world. John 1:1-5 declares, "In the beginning was the Word, and the Word was with God, and the Word was God. The same was in the beginning with God. All things were

BREAD THAT SATISFIES

made by him; and without him was not any thing made that was made. In him was life; and the life was the light of men. And the light shineth in darkness; and the darkness comprehended it not."

John 1:14 states, "And the Word was made flesh, and dwelt among us, and we beheld his glory." We didn't just see a man, a prophet, or a healer. We didn't just see a miracle worker or a water walker. <u>*We saw His glory.*</u>

I picture John, as he was traveling with Jesus during His earthly ministry, being aware of not only what Jesus was doing, but also taking note of <u>who</u> Jesus said He was. Apparently, John paid particular attention to each time Jesus used the words "I am..." It was in John's heart to know Him, so he recorded a number of instances when Jesus revealed Himself with the words "I am..."

- John 4:26—"I am the Messiah."
- John 6:35—"I am the bread of life."
- John 8:23—"I am from above."
- John 8:58—"I am the eternal one."
- John 9:5—"I am the bread of life."
- John 10:7—"I am the door of the sheep."
- John 10:14—"I am the good shepherd."
- John 10:36—"I am the Son of God."
- John 11:25—"I am the resurrection, and the life."
- John 13:13 – "I am the Lord, I am the Master."
- John 14:6—"I am the way, the truth, and the life."
- John 15:1 – "I am the true vine, and my Father is the husbandman."

John continued to write about the person of Jesus in the Book of Revelation.

- Revelation 1:8—"I am Alpha and Omega."
- Revelation 1:17—"I am the first and the last."

- Revelation 19:16, "There was a name written on His vesture, and on His thigh, 'KING OF KINGS, AND LORD OF LORDS.'"

King of Kings and Lord of Lords

John wrote, "We beheld His glory." John had laid hold of something. He didn't just write about what Jesus did. John saw the glory, the King. Jesus is called the King of the Ages (Revelation 15:3) and the King of the Jews. (John 19:19) He's called the King of Israel (John 12:13), the King of the Saints (Revelation 15:3), and the King of Righteousness. (Hebrews 7:2) He's called the King of Glory (Psalm 24:8) and the King of Heaven. (Daniel 4:37) Indeed, He is the KING OF KINGS, and the LORD OF LORDS. (Revelation 19:16) Have you beheld His glory?

CHAPTER 6

The Need for Daily Bread

Sometimes I think about what it must have been like to walk with Jesus during His earthly ministry. I believe that every day was an exciting adventure. The disciples must have awakened each day with a sense of excitement and anticipation because they had no idea what was going to happen that day. Jesus lived a different kind of life than any of them had ever known.

Many of the disciples were religious. They had been raised and trained in the religious ways of their forefathers, but when Jesus came along, He showed them an entirely new way of living. They noticed that He was always prepared to deal with anything and everything He encountered. If mercy was needed, He had it. If He encountered someone with a loved one who had died, He had resurrection power. If He was confronted with the antagonistic questions of the religious leaders, He had the wisdom required to deal with them. If little children wanted His time and attention, He had plenty of love to give them. He always had the grace, the compassion, and the power to minister to hurting and needy people. He always had whatever was required to deal with any situation.

The disciples observed that Jesus prayed differently than they prayed. They had religious training and had been taught the things of God, but they noticed that when Jesus prayed, it was as if He was communing and fellowshipping with the heavenly Father. Jesus often prayed in the early morning hours. The disciples would undoubtedly awaken and hear Him talking to God, often calling Him "Father." Sometimes, Jesus would dialogue with His Father all night long. One day, according to Luke 11:1, Philip came to Jesus and effectively asked, "Will You teach us to pray like You pray?" Of course, Jesus was pleased to respond, giving them guidance and instruction so that they could enter into the new way of living that He had demonstrated to them on a daily basis.

A Higher Way

I believe that God wants to teach us, His people, a higher way of living as well. I believe this is a new and different season which will require us to deal with some things we have not experienced in the past. We will need power instantaneously. We will need mercy and grace to meet the needs of people around us. We will need to have love so that we can forgive immediately when someone offends us. Years ago, we sang a chorus based on Chapter 15 of the Gospel of John. The lyrics proclaimed,

> *"I found a new way of living. I found a new life divine.*
> *I have the fruit of the spirit. I'm abiding, abiding in the vine.*
> *Abiding in the vine, abiding in the vine.*
> *Love, joy, health, peace; He has made them mine.*
> *I have prosperity, power, and victory abiding, abiding in the vine."*

Jesus began to teach the disciples about this higher way of living and specifically about prayer. Matthew 6:7-13 contains the secret that Jesus shared which unlocks the kind of life that He lived. Jesus began by saying, "But when ye pray." Please notice He didn't say <u>if</u>. He said <u>when</u>. The issue is not <u>whether</u> we pray; the issue is <u>how</u> we pray. Jesus said, "Use not vain repetitions, as the heathen do; for they think that they shall be heard for their much speaking. Be not ye therefore like unto them; for your Father knoweth what things ye have need of, before ye ask him." (Matthew 6:8) We don't come to God to provide Him with information. He isn't ever shocked or surprised. He doesn't ever say, "Oh really? I didn't know that." He knows all about us and what we are facing in life. It gives me great peace and confidence to know that He always knows. He is omniscient.

Jesus continued, "After this manner therefore pray ye." He did not say "Repeat these words." He said, "After this manner," which means, "Pray in this way (employing these principles). I'm going to reveal to you the way I commune with My Father." Jesus was opening His heart and teaching the disciples, as well as us, the keys necessary to step into a higher way of living.

Our Father

Jesus addressed God the Father as "Our Father." He didn't say "My Father" in this case because He was showing us that when we pray, we should be mindful of the needs of others and not focused only upon our own situation.

The name "Father" implies relationship. Yes, we can call Him God, because He is God. However, we have the privilege of possessing an intimate relationship with Him. As born-again Christians, we are children of God, and therefore God is our Father. God effectively says, "I want you to commune with Me with the understanding that we are related to one another. I have birthed you. You are a part of My family, and I love you. You are My child, and I am your Father."

Which Art in Heaven

Jesus' next phrase was "which art in heaven." We are not only to recognize His body and His person, but also His position. He is high above all. We must be careful in referring to

God with colloquial terms such as "The man upstairs." He is Almighty God. He is our Father in heaven, and He deserves to be honored and to have His position properly acknowledged.

Hallowed Be Thy Name

Jesus' next phrase was "hallowed be thy name." That means God is holy and we should praise Him. Jesus is speaking of praising Him for who He is. It is certainly good for us to thank Him for what He's done, but we enter into the place of communion with our Father by praising Him because He is God. He is Lord. He is above all else.

Please note that thus far in Jesus' prayer, we have honored His spiritual body, recognized His person, acknowledged His position, and declared His praise…and we haven't even asked for anything yet! Sometimes we get things out of order in our prayers. We begin with, "Dear God, I need, I need, I need." Jesus is teaching us about a new way of living – one that is God-focused instead of self-focused. If we grasp and apply Jesus' teaching, it will literally change our lives. We must learn to declare God's praise and glory for who He is, regardless of whether or not we think all of our needs have been met.

Thy Kingdom Come

"Thy kingdom come." Declare His power, His authority, and the fact that there is none like Him. Declare that His kingdom, the Kingdom of God, stands above every kingdom of this world. Revelation 11:15 declares, "The kingdoms of this world shall become the kingdoms of our Lord, and of His Christ; and He shall reign for ever and ever." No kingdom in this world can compare with His kingdom. Declare His authority and power.

Thy Will Be Done In Earth, As It Is In Heaven

"Thy will be done in earth, as it is in heaven." Proverbs 19:21 states, "Many are the plans in a man's heart, but it is the Lord's purpose that prevails." (NIV) God has a perfect plan for each of our lives which we can experience if we simply yield our will to His. May the power and perfection of heaven be demonstrated in our lives here on earth!

Give Us This Day Our Daily Bread

Thus far, in Jesus' prayer, we have recognized His spiritual body, His person, His position, His praise, His authority, and His purpose. Only after all of that, do we come to the place in prayer at which we make our first request to God. "Give us this day our daily bread." Sometimes we think about this bread as referring only to finances. However, we must look beyond that aspect and understand that our needs for today include much more than monetary things. They may include finances, but they go well beyond material needs. We should effectively pray, "Father I don't know what I'm going to face today, but I know that You have whatever I will need to deal with whatever I will face. Father, I ask You to endow me with everything I will need to walk through this day victoriously, fulfilling Your will and purpose for my life." That is the highest way to live!

Jesus exhibited and demonstrated this higher way of living. He always had whatever He needed. If He needed to show mercy, it was there. If He needed wisdom, it was there. If He needed power, it was there. He never had to say to those that were grieving over a dead loved one, "Hold on while I pray all night, then I'll come back and raise your loved one from the dead." He had sufficient bread each day because He received it from His Father daily.

We never know what we will face each day. If we are offended, we will need forgiveness to put the offense behind us quickly. If we receive a phone call from someone who is very sick, we will need to have the compassion and faith to encourage them and pray the prayer of faith with, or over, them. God knows all that we will need before we need it. He knows everything we are going to face today. I say, "Lord, please give me the bread from Your oven that I'm going to need to accomplish Your purpose and live victoriously today. I'm not asking for the week, I'm asking for today. I can't live on yesterday's bread, and I can't draw from tomorrow's bread. In fact, tomorrow morning we're going to have this same conversation, and I'm going to be talking with You about the same thing. I'm going to need the daily bread that You have in the oven for that day."

Living Victoriously

Many have become almost religious about the idea of going to church once or twice a week and expecting to receive all they need for the week from one or two church services. I believe in attending church faithfully, and receiving from God, but I'm speaking of a higher way of living. The Lord is with us every day. He knows what we are going to need each day in order to live that day victoriously. God does not want us to barely survive and simply hold on until the next church service or the next blessing. God wants us to live victoriously and walk all day, every day, in His will, accomplishing great things for His kingdom.

Many people in our world are confused and don't know where to turn or what to do. Many seem to wander in darkness, hoping they will somehow stumble onto the answers they seek, while missing so many important things. The church has the glorious opportunity to be a light in this dark world and to be the salt of the earth. As believers, we have the ability to draw all we need from the Lord in order to be a living epistle, bringing hope to the hopeless and help to the helpless.

A New Way of Living

God is calling us to a higher way of living. We must begin to be the kind of people that He has created us to be. We cannot just talk about it, sing about it, or declare it—we must start living it. The same spirit that was in Jesus without measure is in us as born again believers. When we first step into this new way of living, it can be somewhat frightening because we have been taught, trained, and encouraged to trust in our own abilities and resources. God is saying, "I want you to come higher because what you are going to face will require more than you possess in the natural. It will require more wisdom than you have. It will require more mercy, grace, love, compassion, and power. It will require a dimension beyond what you can learn in school or muster out of your own human intelligence."

He says, "I have bread in the oven for you." We need His bread. Some may call it "walking in the Spirit" or perhaps "being led by the Spirit." We can call it any number of things, but it is really a new way of living by partaking of, and sharing, the bread that our Father gives us each day. We can arise in the morning confident that we will make it through the day victoriously, because He has the bread in the oven that we need for today. He's a wonderful God.

When we understand and apply this truth, we need not face the day in fear or confusion. We need not wonder whether we will be able to cope, whether we will be able to "keep it together," or if we will fall apart. He is our everything. He knows all that we need. He does not lack anything. He is not limited nor hindered in any way. Knowing this, we can abandon our former way of living and step up into a new way of living. We can live each day out of His provision.

A Living Testimony

I believe that if the Body of Christ begins to live this way, we will become a living testimony to the world of a God who is alive, relevant, and who can manifest today. A God who still heals, saves, and sets the captive free. A God who still raises the dead and has mercy on the hurting and the wounded.

The disciples had been trying to live the best they could, but they were living out of their own resources. They realized Jesus had something better than they had. Perhaps they begged Him, "Please Jesus, give us your secret. Tell us why You always have whatever You need to deal with whatever You face." Jesus responded by teaching them how to pray.

We should go to the Father every morning saying, "Lord, I don't know what I'm going to need today. I don't know what I will face, but You do, and You have exactly what I need. Thy will be done in earth as it is in heaven. Please go to Your oven and give me my bread for today."

When God reveals Himself to us, we begin to understand that He is limitless, and we begin to understand that He has everything in the oven that we need. We must first praise Him, because in praise we exalt Him and we remind ourselves that He is above all before we even ask for bread.

Knowing Him through His Names

Since we cannot physically touch God or normally see Him, we must learn about Him through His Word. Before we are prepared to take such a gigantic leap of trust, we must be confident that He is everything we will ever need. We must be assured He loves us and genuinely cares about us. It is important to believe He won't quit on us, even when we fail Him.

Then, we can go to Him and say: "Lord, I have no idea what to order today because I do not yet know what I will face nor with what I must deal. But I'm confident You know the end from the beginning. I'm thankful to know that even before I ask, You know what I will need. I believe there is nothing impossible for You and I'm reassured of that by Your names." Through His names, He reveals to us what He has in His oven.

The primary way that people living in Old Testament times grew to know God was to learn of His character and attributes through His names. God revealed Himself through fourteen different names found in the Old Testament, and in each of those names we can see another aspect of who He is.

- *Elohim.* He is my CREATOR; all things were made by Him. (Found 2,570 times in Old Testament).
- *Adonai.* He is my LORD, MASTER, and OWNER; the One who possesses me. Spelled *L-o-r-d.* (434 times).
- *El-Elyon.* He is The MOST HIGH GOD; none can compare to Him. (28 times).
- *El-Shaddai.* He is my SUPPLIER and SATISFIER who is more than enough. (7 times)
- *Jehovah/Yahweh.* He is the SELF-SUFFICIENT and SELF-EXISTENT ONE. Spelled *L-O-R-D.* (6,519 times)

There are nine different suffixes to the name *Jehovah,* as follows:

- *Jehovah-Jireh.* He is my PROVIDER. (Found 1 time in the Old Testament)
- *Jehovah-M'Kaddesh.* He is my SANCTIFIER; He separates me *from* the world and *to* Him. (2 times)

- *Jehovah-Nissi.* He is my BANNER; He will fight for me. (1 time)
- *Jehovah-Rohi.* He is my SHEPHERD; I shall not want. (1 time)
- *Jehovah-Rophe.* He is my HEALER and my RESTORER. (1 time)
- *Jehovah-Sabaoth.* He is The LORD OF HOSTS; He has battle strategies. (285 times)
- *Jehovah-Shalom.* He is My PEACE; He brings me into harmony with Him. (1 time)
- *Jehovah-Shammah.* He IS THERE; He dwells among His people. (1 time)
- *Jehovah-T`Sidkenu.* He is my RIGHTEOUSNESS; I am in right standing with Him. (2 times)

There are no words to adequately describe God. He is everything, and He has everything. As we learn to pray as Jesus prayed and receive our daily bread from the Father, we will begin to experience an entirely new way of living!

Knowing Him through His Son

As I have studied the Gospels, my attention has been drawn to the many times the phrase "they marveled," or some form thereof, is used in response to the person and ministry of Jesus. For example, it is said of Him by:
- the multitudes (Matthew. 9:8, 9:33, and 15:31),
- the disciples (Matthew 21:20, Mark 8:27),
- the Pharisees and Herodians (Matthew 22:22),
- Pontius Pilate, the governor (Matthew 27:14),
- Joseph and Mary, His mother (Luke 2:33),
- the Jews (John 7:15), and
- the Chief Priests and Scribes (Matthew 21:15).

The word "marvelous" or "marveled" comes from the Greek word "thau-mazo" which means "to gaze in admiration, in wonder, or in awe; to be speechless and spellbound in overwhelming adoration, causing all our faculties to stand at attention!"

Captivated by His ability to deal successfully with whatever He encountered, peoples' reaction clearly declared "He is Awesome!" Many wanted to be near Him to touch Him, listen to Him, and/or to worship Him. They were awed by His power. His grace, love, and mercy were unlike that of any other man. His wisdom and understanding left them speechless. The words that He spoke were like fresh bread directly from heaven.

This should be our daily testimony as well. In our humanness, we must guard against allowing our awe of Him to decline or wane. There is no weakness or disappointment in Him. He never fails nor changes. He is forever awesome! The words of a well known chorus describe the way it ought to be in each of our lives:

> *"The longer I know Him, the sweeter He grows.*
> *The more that I love Him, more love He bestows.*
> *Each day is like heaven, my heart overflows.*
> *The longer I know Him, the sweeter He grows."*

Luke 10:40 speaks of Martha, the sister of Mary and Lazarus, as being "cumbered" (distracted by or over-occupied with) faithfully discharging her duties in life. That becomes a problem only when we detect a waning or declining in our awe of Him.

Matthew 15:8 records Jesus' warning that it is possible to draw near to Him with our mouth, and honor Him with our lips, yet in reality, our heart can be far from Him.

Experiencing a decline of awe in relationships with people or things of this world is common. First time experiences like air travel and making new friendships often fit into that category. Typical dissipation of awe toward a person sounds something like this: "He's awesome...he's wonderful...he's a great guy...he's a good guy...he's pretty good...he's OK...it all depends...he needs prayer...he turns me off...he's hard to tolerate...I can't stand him!"

I believe God wants us to walk in His awesomeness on a daily basis as opposed to a lifestyle of simply seeking a spiritual "high" or "fix" occasionally in a "blowout" church service. When we lose our awe of Him, we often must be motivated to serve Him out of guilt or fear. Such motivation is not effective, lasting, nor pleasing to Him. Service as an act of love and worship is the only enduring and rewarding way. (Matthew 4:10)

Words alone are inadequate to describe the glory of our Savior, Lord, and King, but as we humbly bow before Him and seek His provision (bread) for each day, we will experience an abundant life of joy, effectiveness, and fulfillment. (John 10:10) Walking daily with Him is truly the bread that satisfies.

CHAPTER 7

Returning to the House of Bread

Naomi and her husband Elimelech lived in Judah, in the town of Bethlehem, which means "the house of bread." When famine struck their region, they and their two sons Mahlon and Chilion moved to the country of Moab. After some time, Elimelech died. Naomi's two sons married Moabite women, and the entire family dwelt in Moab. Some time later, Mahlon and Chilion also died. Naomi, a Judean, was left there in Moab with her Moabite daughters-in-law, who were named Orpah and Ruth. Word came to Naomi that the famine in Judah had ended, so she decided to return to her homeland. She kissed her two daughters-in-law, bade them farewell, and turned to depart.

Orpah and Ruth responded to Naomi's goodbye in very different ways. Their responses are recorded in Ruth 1:14-18, which states, "And they lifted up their voice, and wept again; and Orpah <u>kissed</u> her mother in law. But Ruth <u>clave</u> unto her. And she <Naomi> said, Behold, thy sister-in-law is gone back unto her people, and unto her gods. And Ruth said, Intreat me not to leave thee, or to return from following after thee; for whither thou goest, I will go; and where thou lodgest, I will lodge; thy people shall be my people, and thy God my God. Where thou diest, will I die, and there will I be buried; the Lord do so to me, and more also, if ought but death part thee and me. When she saw that she was steadfastly minded to go with her, she left <ceased> speaking unto her."

Please note that Orpah <u>kissed</u> Naomi, but Ruth <u>clung</u> to her. Orpah was a "kisser," but Ruth was a "cleaver." The name "Naomi" means "the pleasantness of Jehovah." The name "Orpah" means "double-minded, stiff necked, or stubborn." The name "Ruth" means "a true and lasting friend." While Orpah's relationship to Naomi was one of external affection expressed in a kiss, Ruth's association with Naomi was one of total commitment that involved her complete lifestyle. Ruth was not satisfied to identify with Naomi in an externally affectionate way. Instead, she effectively said to Naomi, "I want to live my life with you. The place of my dwelling will be wherever you dwell. The people that are your friends will be my friends, and I gladly forsake all other gods and make your God my God. This commitment is not just for today – it is until death. Wherever you die, that's where I'll die and be buried. We have come into a covenant relationship and I am determined to live out the implications of that covenant. I give myself wholly to you and your ways."

This is the beginning of a very powerful story that illustrates the relationship that we are to have with our Lord Jesus Christ. In this story is a foreshadowing and type of the greatest thing that has ever happened to the human race. The most incredible story of the Bible is that Almighty God, the Creator of all things, would make covenant with man through Jesus Christ. He reached out to us and cut a blood covenant which dramatically affects us as we respond with all our hearts. We cannot wholly understand nor fully appreciate the Word of God unless we understand covenant. In our Western culture, we have not had much teaching, training, or experience on the subject of "covenant." Perhaps the closest thing we can relate to covenant is when we celebrate the union of a man and woman in holy matrimony, signifying a spiritual union and total commitment to each other. However, even in that context, our society has minimized the marriage covenant to the point that, in the minds of many people, it's nothing more than a legal agreement. However, true biblical covenant involves forsaking all others and wholly committing oneself, without reservation, to the other until death.

In this context, Jesus introduced the "new covenant." Chapters 13 and 14 of the Gospel of John relate the account of Jesus at the Last Supper. Everything that is recorded in those two chapters took place at the table that night. It was obviously important to Jesus that He convey certain truths and principles to the disciples before they left the upper room. In other words, there are implications to identification with the Lord's Supper that involve more than just receiving the bread and cup. There are implications to identifying with His table and with the new covenant.

Receiving What He Has Given

The Apostle Paul reminds us that the bread and the cup were given by the Lord. (I Corinthians 11) Therefore, the early part of this special meal, which Jesus greatly desired to eat with His disciples, involved each of them receiving from Him. As He took the bread, He said "this is my body, which is broken for you." And, "After the same manner also he took the cup, when he had supped, saying, 'This cup is the new covenant in my blood.'" Matthew 26:27 states that Jesus said, "Drink ye all of it." So He encouraged them to "eat" and "drink," and receive what He was giving.

All eyes were on Jesus. All attention was focused upon Him. He was foreshadowing what He was going to live out over the next several hours by going to the cross and shedding His blood. This was God making covenant with man through Christ Jesus, the head of a new race, the head of a new covenant by which you and I could come into the family of God. They were celebrating that covenant, and that is what we do when we celebrate communion. Jesus said, "Take, eat: this is my body, which is broken for you: this do in remembrance of me." Then, "After the same manner also he took the cup, when he had supped, saying, This cup is the new testament in my blood: this do ye, as oft as ye drink it, in remembrance of me.." (I Corinthians 11:24-25) Every blood covenant was consummated with a memorial, often a meal. Jesus gave that to us so that we would remember that we are in covenant with Him.

Going Beyond Receiving

After the disciples received the bread and the cup, Jesus continued to share with them that there are more implications to covenant than just receiving from Him. Jesus began to say and do things that were even more difficult for His disciples to understand. He washed their feet and gave them a new commandment that is associated with the new covenant. It pertained only to the people that had received the bread and the cup – covenant people. There were certain things Jesus spoke to the multitudes. There were certain miracles He did for all the people that came to Him. However, there were other things that were reserved just for people that were in covenant. There are implications of entering into covenant and of identifying with covenant. This is important to see, because I believe that as we continue to grow in this truth it will transform our lives and our walk with Him.

It's not very difficult for our human nature to learn to receive from God. We are all born into this world with a tendency to grasp everything we can – we are "graspers" by nature. However, the implications of the covenant deal with things that our human nature doesn't naturally do. Jesus declared, "A new commandment I give unto you." (John 13:34) To whom was

Jesus referring when He used the word "you?" He was referring to those who have identified with the bread and the cup. "That ye love one another; as I have loved you, that ye also love one another. By this shall all men know that ye are my disciples, if ye have love one *to* another." (John 13:35)

Jesus came with the basin and towel, washed the disciples' feet, and instructed them to do likewise. Then He told them that there is a new commandment associated with the new covenant—love one another even as He has loved them. We don't have a great deal of difficulty loving Jesus because He is majestic, wonderful, glorious, and marvelous. We don't have difficulty identifying with His broken body by receiving the bread or identifying with His blood by receiving the cup. However, the covenant goes beyond that. Jesus said the implications of covenant involve not just our relationship with Him, but also our relationship with our fellow believers as the spiritual body of Christ. Jesus is the head, and we are the members of Christ's body. The implications of covenant are not only that we honor and worship the head, but that we cleave to, and identify with, His body.

Covenant Living

Judas Iscariot was a kisser. He walked into the Garden of Gethsemane and kissed Jesus, but he was not living out the implications of covenant. Judas received the bread and the cup, but he left just before Jesus' commandment to love and serve one another. We must not be like Judas, but instead we should realize that there are implications that make demands upon us as covenant people. If we believe the covenant and identify with what Christ has done, it has implications upon our lifestyle. A Christian must not live like the world lives. The covenant affects how we live, how we talk, how we think, and how we act. It's important that we see this. Some people think that Christianity is all about praying a prayer which assures they won't go to hell. Jesus is talking about something much deeper and more glorious than that, which involves knowing Him, walking in His presence, and understanding all that He has provided through the covenant. He wants us to have the joy, the peace, the life, the power, the strength, the wisdom, and all that we need because we're in covenant with Him.

It's more difficult to live out the implications of the covenant with our brothers and sisters than it is with Him. Some might think, "It's just Jesus and me, and we're having a good time until He returns." However, we cannot exclude others. There is no way to do that scripturally because we are the Body of Christ. I owe something to you, you owe something to me. Every gift that God gives us belongs to the Body of Christ. Every gift He gives is meant to be shared.

Learning about Love

When I was a young boy, I didn't fully understand the implications of covenant. I thought I understood what Jesus meant when He said "Love one another," but I came to discover that I didn't even understand the word "love." I had a relationship with my teddy bear that I really enjoyed. He was brown and had little black ears, a chubby nose, and a red tongue. He had a grin on his face, and his arms were always outstretched. He was very fluffy, loveable, and kissable. I enjoyed him, and we had some good times together. I loved my teddy bear, and I would hug and kiss him. I would put him on the couch and preach to him, and he smiled all the way through the sermon. When I would finish, he was still smiling. No matter what I did to him, he would smile. As a boy, I was a restless sleeper who apparently tossed and turned frequently in my sleep. I would take my teddy bear to bed with me at night. Many mornings when I awoke, my teddy bear was on the floor. I would pick him up and he would still be smiling. When I went out to play, I would put him on the couch and when I came back he was still there, always smiling. I thought the relationship that my teddy bear and I shared was love.

However, I outgrew my teddy bear, eventually met a beautiful young woman, and entered into a marriage covenant with her. Only then did I begin to truly understand covenant. I began to understand that it meant more than a kiss. My wife is wonderful, but I soon learned that she didn't always react to me the way my teddy bear did. She didn't always smile. I'd go to work and leave her on the couch and when I returned home she had moved. I began to understand that it wasn't like with my relationship with my teddy bear, because my teddy bear existed to please me. Whenever I wanted to, I could put him on the shelf. Whenever I wanted to play with him, I would play with him. However, in marriage, I began to understand that I had a commitment to uphold, and there were implications to the covenant I had made. When I committed to give her everything I have and ever shall have, everything I am and ever shall be, there were implications. Jesus turned to His disciples and effectively said, "I want you to understand covenant. You're not going to have much trouble loving Me, but I want you to know that covenant love doesn't only go one way (receiving), but it also requires giving and commitment on your part."

Jesus gives us an analogy when He says to love "as I have loved you." John 13:1 declares that "the Father, having loved his own which were in the world, he loved them unto the end." There is something very important here. Jesus doesn't want us to simply admire His lifestyle. He wants us to emulate Him. He said that the world will know that we are in covenant with

Him because of our example of love to one another. We have a responsibility to each other when we are in covenant with Him.

We are family. I believe that as the Body of Christ understands and embraces our commitment to each other in a greater way, God is pleased and people are blessed. I believe we all have special giftings from God. Many have anointings and giftings they haven't yet discovered. I've seen some people who are so full of the love of Jesus and the joy of the Lord that everyone they touch is affected by their love, attitude, and actions. Lord, help us to cleave to You, and to each other, as You intended for us to do. Help us to be cleavers, not simply kissers!

CHAPTER 8

The Odor of the House

In this chapter, we will examine a worship experience that Jesus said would be spoken of throughout the whole world wherever the gospel is preached. It is recorded in three of the gospels (Matthew, Mark, and John). We will study the account which is found in John's gospel.

John 12:1-11 declares, "Then Jesus six days before the Passover came to Bethany, where Lazarus was which had been dead, whom he raised from the dead. There they made him a supper, and Martha served; but Lazarus was one of them that sat at the table with him. Then took Mary a pound of ointment of spikenard, very costly, and anointed the feet of Jesus, and wiped his feet with her hair; and the house was filled with the odour of the ointment. Then saith one of his disciples, Judas Iscariot, Simon's son, which should betray him, Why was not this ointment sold for three hundred pence, and given to the poor? This he said, not that he cared for the poor; but because he was a thief, and had the bag, and bare what was put therein. Then said Jesus, Let her alone; against the day of my burying hath she kept this. For the poor always ye have with you; but me ye have not always. Much people of the Jews therefore knew that he was there; and they came not for Jesus' sake only, but that they might see Lazarus also, whom he had raised from the dead. But the chief priests consulted that they might put Lazarus also to death. Because that by reason of him many of the Jews went away, and believed on Jesus."

Please note that the last part of verse 3 states, *"and the house was filled with the odour of the ointment."*

The Gathering

This event took place in the little village of Bethany, not long before Jesus' death. Bethany was about two miles southeast of Jerusalem on the eastern slope of the Mount of Olives. This event took place in the house of a man named Simon. Most theologians believe that Simon, who had been a leper but now was whole, was healed through the power of God during the earthly ministry of our Lord Jesus Christ. The Word of God says that they planned a great supper and invited many important people including Jesus, His disciples, and Lazarus, whom Jesus had raised from the dead.

If you were to enter the room that night, the first thing that would catch your attention would be the aroma of Middle-Eastern foods. The people had gathered for supper and Martha was preparing to serve. As the people mingled and conversed, undoubtedly the resurrection of Lazarus was the center of conversation, as it would be if we were to attend such a gathering today.

I can imagine some of the questions that may have been raised. "Lazarus, can you tell us about this experience? What was it like when you died? Did you feel like you were going through a tunnel? Did you see a bright light? Did you see anyone you recognized? How did it feel when suddenly you were back in your body still wrapped in grave clothes?"

The Precious Ointment and the Unseen Worshipper

While informal conversation was transpiring and food was being prepared for the supper, the Word of God tells us a woman by the name of Mary slipped into the room unceremoniously, uninvited, and unnoticed. Scripture says she was carrying an alabaster box. The term "alabaster box" comes from the Greek word *alabastron* which identifies a container that carried very precious ointment. The container had a conical shape and the ointment it contained was so precious that its value was worth a year's wages. The container's lid was sealed with wax and wrapped with twine to keep the fragrance from escaping. The ointment was made from a root plant called *nard* which grew in a far off place that we now know as India. It was very precious ointment, processed and shipped hundreds of miles to the vicinity of Jerusalem. Even today, nard is found in only four countries in the world – India, China, Turkey, and Greece. The root of the plant has a very delightful aroma.

As Mary walked into the room unnoticed, she slipped over to where Jesus was sitting. She had no difficulty getting near Jesus, perhaps because most people were gathered around Lazarus and Simon listening to their stories. When she got to Jesus, she broke the container (literally translated, she broke the seal of the container), and then she began to pour the very precious nard upon Jesus' head and beard. The ointment flowed down over His garments, saturating them, and its fragrance permeated the room. Then, in a very striking act, she dropped to her knees and began pouring the remaining nard on His feet. She then let down her hair and wiped His feet with it, cleaning off the dirt and grime that would often cling to the feet of people as they walked in sandals on the dusty roads in that day. As she knelt there in this deep act of love, humility, and worship, she emptied her nard on Jesus. The Word of God says, "*And the house was filled with the odour of the ointment.*" I call that true worship. I call that worshipping "in spirit and in truth." (John 4:24)

Of all our senses, the sense of smell is perhaps the most sensitive to our surroundings. As she poured the ointment, it wasn't long before others that were in attendance began to smell the odor. It is a very pervasive and penetrating odor, capable even of overpowering the odor of the aromatic Middle-Eastern foods that were being prepared for the supper. The people traced the smell to where Jesus was. As they drew near to Him, they were astonished at the sight of Mary pouring precious ointment on His feet and wiping His feet with her hair. Many of them were offended and scandalized, and they began to complain to one another. "What is she doing interrupting this supper and all the plans that we have made?" Some of them became very angry. Judas spoke out and effectively said, "This is terrible. This is an absolute waste. That ointment could have been sold for three hundred pence and given to the poor." In spite of all the scandal and unhappiness on the part of the guests, Mary was unfazed. She continued her act of love and worship despite all of the naysayers.

Worship Him for Who He Is

After a short while, as their anger, criticism, and cynicism continued, Jesus spoke out and said, "Let her alone; against the day of my burying hath she kept this." Please note that after Jesus died and His body was taken down from the cross, Joseph of Arimathea brought a hundred pounds of nard to pour on His body to prepare the body for burial. Yet, there isn't one word of praise in the Bible concerning Joseph's gift of one hundred pounds of nard given after Jesus' death. Rather, the Bible commends the woman who brought only one pound of nard, but did so <u>before</u> His death and burial. She was pouring out the ointment in a beautiful expression of heartfelt worship. The people had gathered to talk to Simon and Lazarus. *They had gathered to talk about what Jesus had done but she came to worship who He is.* She poured and poured and poured. I believe that the Lord is showing us through this story that it is important that we give honor to whom honor is due while they are still able to receive it.

There was another one at the table that night that was very much like Mary. His name was John, and he was a unique disciple. His gospel causes us to understand that He was always interested in who Jesus was. He was undoubtedly grateful for everything Jesus did, but while everyone else was "oohing and ahhing" over the miracles, John was listening every time that Jesus would talk about who He was. Every once in a while Jesus would make the statement "I Am." In my mind's eye, to modernize it, I see John with his notebook, and whenever Jesus made the statement "I Am," John wrote it down. As he did so, there was a progressive revelation of Jesus Christ, and he was understanding more and more about who He was. I can imagine John saying, "Oh yes, it is wonderful what He's doing, but I'm captivated more by who He is." Jesus revealed Himself many times by using the words "I am."

- "I am the Messiah." (John 4:26)
- "I am the bread of life." (John 6:35)
- "I am from above." (John 8:23)
- "I am the eternal one." (John 8:58)
- "I am the light of the world." (John 9:5)
- "I am the door of the sheepfold." (John 10:7)
- "I am the good shepherd." (John 10:14)
- "I am the Son of God." (John 10:36)
- "I am the resurrection, and the life." (John 11:25)
- "I am the Lord and the Master." (John 13:13)
- "I am the way, the truth, and the life." (John 14:6)

- "I am the true vine, and my Father is the husbandman." (John 15:1)

He carries it into the book of Revelation.

- "I am Alpha and Omega, the beginning and the ending." (Revelation 1:8)
- "I am the first and the last." (Revelation 1:17)
- "And he hath on his vesture and on his thigh a name written, King of Kings, and Lord of Lords." (Revelation 19:16)

It's who He is that matters above all else. What He does comes out of who He is. We thank Him for what He's done, but we praise Him for who He is. We worship Him as we pour our lives, our love, our "nard," on Him.

The Smell of Worship

That night when the supper was over, two people left the room smelling of nard. One was Mary. She had been pouring nard, and it had spilled all over her. She carried the smell of her worship, the fragrance of the nard. I can see her as she went out into the street after the meeting. Mary lived in Bethany, so she left Simon's house and walked toward her house down the street, her hair oily, dirty and matted. Perhaps a passerby asked, "Mary, what happened to you?"

Have you ever been there? Have you ever been driving down the street and the presence of the Lord fills your car? Have you ever been lying in bed at night when the Word of God begins to fill your heart, or the Spirit of the Lord causes a song to rise up within you? In response, your tears begin to flow. Worship can get messy. Have you been there? Your eyes become red and swollen. You may have had your hair fixed yesterday but you would never know it today. Mary had been with Jesus. She had been touched by Him. She poured everything she had, and everything

BREAD THAT SATISFIES

she was, on Him. It was _who He was_ that captivated her. Others may have been standing off to the side talking about what He had done, but it's _who He was_ that thrilled her heart. She poured and said, "He is worth all of my nard – every last drop."

The lyrics of a well known song contain the words, "When I think about the Lord, how He saved me, how He raised me, how He filled me with the Holy Ghost, how He healed me to the uttermost..." I can't help but love Him. I can't help but yield myself wholly to Him. I can't help but follow Him. I worship Him with every step I take, every day I live, and every breath I breathe. _It's all because of who He is._

A Good God

God is a good God. Acts 10:38 states, "How God anointed Jesus of Nazareth with the Holy Ghost and with power; who went about doing good, and healing all that were oppressed of the devil." Hebrews 13:8 declares that He is "the same yesterday, today, and forever." He is a good God. He still saves sinners. He still restores backsliders. He still heals the sick. He still sets the captive free. He still raises the dead. He still strengthens the weak. He still lifts up the fallen. He still blesses the children. He still rewards the faithful. He is a good God!

A Mighty God

He's also a mighty God. David wrote in Psalm 24:8, "Who is this King of glory? The Lord strong and mighty, the Lord mighty in battle." He's so big our minds can't contain Him. He's so strong our hands can't restrain Him. We can't outlive Him, and we can't live without Him. The Pharisees couldn't stand Him. The Sadducees couldn't stop Him. Pilate couldn't find any fault in Him. The witnesses couldn't agree against Him. Herod couldn't kill Him. Death couldn't handle Him, and the grave couldn't hold Him. He is a mighty God!

A Great God

He is also a <u>great</u> God. Psalm 48:1-2 declares, "<u>Great</u> is the Lord, and greatly to be praised in the city of our God, in the mountain of his holiness. Beautiful for situation, the joy of the whole earth, is mount Zion, on the sides of the north, the city of the great King." He is indestructible. He is incorruptible. He is incomparable. He is incomprehensible. He is indispensable. He is indivisible. He is indescribable. He is inexhaustible. He is infallible. He is immutable. He is invincible. He is omnipresent, omniscient, and omnipotent. He is a good, a great, and a mighty God!

The Centurion's Story

Jesus was the other person that left Simon's house that night smelling of nard. A few days later, He was arrested in the Garden of Gethsemane and taken to Pilate's judgment hall. He carried His cross on the Via Delarosa, the way of sorrows, all the way to Golgotha.

After Jesus died, the centurion and the other soldiers returned to their homes. As the centurion arrived home, perhaps the dialogue with his wife transpired somewhat as follows. "Honey, I saw a crucifixion today that was unlike any crucifixion I've ever seen in my life. There was a different man on each of three crosses, but it was the one on the middle cross that really caught my attention. I couldn't take my eyes off of Him. There was something totally different about Him. I've never seen a man die with such dignity, such self control. In all of my years, I've never witnessed anything like it. The people that gathered were cruel. They walked by His cross and screamed obscenities at Him. They cursed Him, laughing and mocking. I heard one of them shout, 'If you're the Son of God, come down from the cross!' The chief priests were saying, 'If you're the King of the Jews, save yourself. He saved others, but He cannot save Himself!' It was terrible, but He never cursed them in return. In His tear-filled eyes I could see compassion and love. You should have been there. I couldn't take my eyes off Him."

He continued, "There were a few times when He spoke to someone whom He called Father. He said things like, 'Father forgive them for they know not what they do' and 'Lay not this sin to their charge.' I couldn't believe it. Toward the end He looked up again and said, 'Father, into thy hands I commend my spirit.' A few short minutes later, He lifted His head for the last time and shouted out over the hillside, 'It is finished.' When He said that, the earth began to shake. It was followed by an eerie silence. The birds quit singing and the wind quit blowing and the sun hid its face. It was then, at that moment...I knew...I was certain...He was the Son of God. We have crucified The Son of God!"

About that time, the centurion's wife asked, "What's that smell? What are you carrying?" He replied, "When He was crucified, we divided His garments. But when we came to His robe we chose not to divide it because it was seamless. We cast lots for it and I won it." At that point he lifted the garment and said, "Isn't it beautiful, Honey? Isn't it beautiful?" And one more time, *the house was filled with the odor of the ointment*.

We Each Have a Bottle of Nard

Every one of us was born with "a bottle of nard." We have one life which we can choose to pour out on Jesus. We have been given love, time, talents, and resources. We each have a bottle of nard.

The people at Simon's house must have been wondering what Mary was thinking, since normally the bottle of nard was kept for "<u>the</u> man," not just any man. It was reserved for when the young lady would meet "<u>the</u> man" in her life. That's who Jesus was to Mary: He was "<u>the</u> man." When she met Jesus, she took her costly nard, broke the seal, and poured it all on Him—every last drop! As she poured it on Him, it also spilled all over her, and as others came near her, they could smell it and they knew that she had been with Jesus.

I love the lyrics of the song "I Surrender All" which say in part, "All to Thee my blessed Savior, I surrender all." That's the testimony of my life. I have only one life to live. I almost lost my life when I was three years old. Three doctors told my parents to prepare for my funeral. However, my parents learned of a church that believed in divine healing. They carried my limp, dying body to that little storefront church, and God miraculously and instantaneously put a new set of lungs in my body. I intend to spend my entire life, until either Jesus returns or He calls me home, pouring my worship on Him, because there's no one like Jesus. He's "<u>the</u> man," the one that poured out His life for us. All He asks in return is that we give ours back to Him.

It doesn't matter what everyone else in the room is doing or what they are all talking about. It doesn't make any difference what seems to occupy others' thoughts and desires for the future. Simply work your way through the crowd, bow your knee at His feet, and pour your life out on Him. When you do, you'll carry the odor of worship wherever you go. You may look a little different. People may ask you why you act the way you do. They may even ask of the hope that lies in you. (I Peter 3:15) You can tell them, "I met '<u>the</u> man.' I met Jesus, and I surrendered all."

CHAPTER 9

Honoring His Presence

The account of the death of Uzzah is one of the most controversial and puzzling stories in the Bible. However, I believe that it contains many important truths that we can apply to our lives, especially in the area of honoring the presence of God. The story of Uzzah, and the return of the Ark of the Covenant to Jerusalem, is recorded in II Samuel 6:1-13, which reads as follows, "Again, David gathered together all the chosen men of Israel, thirty thousand. And David arose, and went with all the people that were with him from Baale of Judah, to bring up from thence the ark of God, whose name is called by the name of the LORD of hosts that dwelleth between the cherubim. And they set the ark of God upon a new cart, and brought it out of the house of Abinadab that was in Gibeah: and Uzzah and Ahio, the sons of Abinadab, drave the new cart. And they brought it out of the house of Abinadab which was at Gibeah, accompanying the ark of God: and Ahio went before the ark. And David and all the house of Israel played before the LORD on all manner of instruments made of fir wood, even on harps, and on psalteries, and on timbrels, and on cornets, and on cymbals."

"And when they came to Nachon's threshing floor, Uzzah put forth his hand to the ark of God, and took hold of it; for the oxen shook it. And the anger of the LORD was kindled against Uzzah; and God smote him there for his error; and there he died by the ark of God. And David was displeased, because the

LORD had made a breach upon Uzzah: and he called the name of the place Perezuzzah to this day. And David was afraid of the LORD that day, and said, How shall the ark of the LORD come to me? So David would not remove the ark of the LORD unto him into the city of David: but David carried it aside into the house of Obededom the Gittite. And the ark of the LORD continued in the house of Obededom the Gittite three months: and the LORD blessed Obededom, and all his household. And it was told king David, saying, The LORD hath blessed the house of Obededom, and all that pertaineth unto him, because of the ark of God. So David went and brought up the ark of God from the house of Obededom into the city of David with gladness. And it was so, that when they that bare the ark of the LORD had gone six paces, he sacrificed oxen and fatlings."

The Ark of the Covenant
When God gave Moses the specifications for the Tabernacle, He not only told him how the Tabernacle should be designed—with the Outer Court, the Holy Place, and the Holiest of Holies—but He also gave specific instructions concerning the furniture that was to be placed in the Tabernacle. (Exodus 25:10-22) The Holiest of Holies, the most sacred, high holy place of all, contained only one piece of furniture—the Ark of the Covenant.

The Ark, which means "box" or "chest," was made of acacia wood and was rectangular in shape, approximately 3 3/4 feet long and 2 1/4 feet wide and high. It was gold plated inside and out with a gold border or crown molding. It was supported by a gold ring on each of the four corners into which carrying poles of gold plated acacia wood were permanently inserted. The lid of pure gold was called the "mercy seat," which means the place of "propitiatory atonement." At its two ends and facing each other were two hammered gold cherubim with wings overshadowing the lid and with their faces pointed toward the middle.

Recorded in Exodus 25:22, God said: "And there I will meet with thee, and I will commune with thee from above the mercy seat, from between the two cherubims which are upon the ark of the testimony." God made mention of that again in II Samuel 6:2 when He identified Himself as "the Lord of hosts that dwelleth between the cherubims." His Person, His Presence was there.

Four Levels of the Presence of God

Upon examination of the Scriptures, we discover that there are four levels of the presence of God. The first level is His <u>omnipresence</u>. He is literally everywhere present. There is no place where God is not.

The second level, and one that is very important to believers, is called His <u>indwelling presence</u>. When we are born again, our spirit is regenerated, we are made spiritually alive, and He lives in us.

The third level is called the <u>manifest presence</u> of God, which is when He chooses to express Himself in some unusual or miraculous way. He can do this at any place and time of His choosing, but I have observed that He often manifests His presence in the midst of an atmosphere of praise, worship, or prayer. In such an atmosphere, I have witnessed people instantaneously healed or set free from various types of bondage. Sometimes the Holy Spirit's convicting power is so great that unbelievers reach out to God to be saved without waiting for an invitation.

The fourth level is called the abiding presence or the <u>Shekinah glory</u> of God, and it is where God chooses to manifest His presence in an unusual way over a prolonged period of time.

He Dwells In Us

We must understand that under the new covenant, because we have been washed in the blood of Jesus, God can now come and dwell in us. We don't look to a box anymore, but we praise God for the fact that He has moved into us. His indwelling presence and abiding presence is within us. Jesus said about us, "If ye abide in me, and my words abide in you, ye shall ask what ye will, and it shall be done unto you." (John 15:7) He used the illustration of the vine and the branches and He effectively said, "I have moved into you, and I'm here to glorify Myself in you and through you so that I may accomplish My purpose."

Bringing Back the Ark

After his capture of Jerusalem in 1003 B.C., King David decided to have the Ark brought to his new capital as an act of respect for the person and presence of God. The Ark had been in the house of Abinadab for some time following the disaster it had brought to several Philistine cities. The two sons of Abinadab, Uzzah and Ahio, were driving the cart upon which the Ark of the Covenant had been placed. At the threshing floor of Nacon, either the oxen stumbled or the Ark began to slide, and Uzzah reached out to steady the Ark. As a result, God was displeased and Uzzah was smitten. The Hebrew word indicates that God actually became angry.

If we rely only upon our human sense of justice and fairness, we could become troubled thinking that Uzzah's death was an unjust and overly severe consequence of his apparent attempt to prevent damage to the Ark. However, something of a much more serious nature obviously angered God. I suggest there are at least three things borne out by this account that shed light upon what brought God's displeasure.

BREAD THAT SATISFIES

Displeasing the Lord: Compromise

The first thing that brought God's displeasure is found in II Samuel 6:3-4 which states, "They set the ark of God upon a new cart, and brought it out of the house of Abinadab that was in Gibeah; and Uzzah and Ahio, and the sons of Abinadab, drave the new cart. And they brought it out of the house of Abinadab which was at Gibeah, accompanying the ark of God; and Ahio went before the ark." Their first transgression was placing the Ark on a new cart. That was unacceptable because the practice of transporting the Ark on a cart came from the Philistines, not from God. They were effectively treating the person and presence of God in the same disrespectful way that the ungodly Philistines had done. God had clearly given instructions that whenever the Ark was to be transported, it was to be carried on the shoulders of the Levites, the priests. (Numbers 4:1-15, I Chronicles 15:2) The priests were to be the leaders in carrying the person, presence, and power of the Lord. Clearly, the Israelites transgressed by compromising God's Word and doing things the way the ungodly did. They attempted to carry God's presence on a "cart of compromise."

We must honor and obey God and His Word whether it's popular or not. *God's presence will never, ever, be carried by "carts." It will only be carried by anointed priests.* The Word of God tells us that we can't walk in compromise. John wrote in his first epistle, "Love not the world, neither the things that are in the world. If any man love the world, the love of the Father is not in him." (I John 2:15) The Holy Spirit, through the pen of John, was saying, "Love not the world's system." The world's system does not please God. This was the first thing that brought the displeasure of God. Today it doesn't always bring physical death, as it did to Uzzah, but it often brings spiritual death. You can find yourself having pleasure in the world but dying spiritually in the process. We can describe the first mistake with the word "compromise."

Displeasing the Lord: Familiarity

A second thing which displeased the Lord is found in II Samuel 6:4, which declares, "They brought it out of the house of Abinadab which was at Gibeah, accompanying the ark of God; and Ahio went before the ark." This is very interesting because we know, upon careful study, that the Ark was in the house of Abinadab for about twenty years. When we have a piece of furniture in our house for twenty years, we may have a tendency to walk by it and ignore it. We may not even look at it nor think anything about it. Perhaps we don't even dust it anymore. It becomes so familiar to us that it loses its importance and becomes just another piece of furniture. We can describe this second mistake with the word "familiarity."

We can learn all the words to all of the hymns and worship choruses, yet not truly worship God. We can memorize Scripture and yet it can be meaningless to us. We can sit in a church service and not even be stirred spiritually anymore. When we lose the awesomeness of the person and the presence of God, we've lost everything. When the name of Jesus doesn't thrill us like it once did, we are spiritually dying. When the Word of God doesn't challenge us, and our hunger for Him and for His Word isn't as intense as it once was, we are in serious spiritual trouble.

My first airplane flight was an incredible experience. I didn't sleep much the night before the flight. I boarded the plane and never slept for a moment throughout the flight. My eyes were wide open and I was taking everything in, and listening to every noise. However, when I board an airplane now, I often go to sleep before we take off. Why? Because I have become familiar with the entire process.

That's okay in the natural but not in the spiritual. We need to say, "Lord, don't let Your name ever become just another word to me. Don't let Your Word ever become just another book to me. Don't let me lose the thrill of singing about Your goodness, glory, and grace."

Displeasing the Lord: Self-Sufficiency

Thirdly, we must be wary of self-sufficiency. The word "Uzzah" means "I am strong." It speaks of an independent spirit, of a person that considers himself sufficient without God. This is the very sin that tempted Adam and Eve in the garden. The serpent told them that they could be like gods. He told them that they could know good from evil, and in effect, that they didn't need God. There is a spirit of independence in the world that is anti-God.

However, I believe the closer we get to God, the more dependent we become upon Him. The word "Uzzah" defies that whole attitude of dependence. It says, "I am strong, I can do it. I can handle anything." Over my many years of life and ministry, I have learned a few things, and one of the most important things I have learned is that I need Him desperately. I want to be dependent upon Him. I don't want Him to be an accessory in my life. I want Him to be the core, the center, of my life. He is the direction and help that we all need.

In order to avoid spiritual death, we must be careful how we interact with the Lord. I believe this is why the Holy Spirit recorded the account of Uzzah in the Bible. This doesn't suggest that God is unjust. He didn't want to cut them off. He wanted the Ark to come back into the midst of His people. While the Ark was in the house of Abinadab, God blessed that household, and David said, "I'm going to get the Ark because the blessing resides in the presence and person of God. We need it. We can't do without it." Likewise, we can't do without His presence in our personal lives.

Cherish Him

Worship shouldn't be limited to the occasions when believers gather. It should be a part of our personal lifestyle. We should get up in the morning, glorify the Lord, praise Him, worship Him, and thank Him for His presence. We should cherish the privilege of worshipping Him. I love the lyrics to the chorus of "The Old Rugged Cross" which say,

> *"I will cherish the old rugged cross, till my trophies at last I lay down.*
> *I will cling to the old rugged cross, and exchange it someday for a crown."*

Many people have abandoned the message of the cross. Many don't want to talk about the blood of Jesus or the name of Jesus anymore. The religious leaders came against the early church and effectively said to the apostles, "We will let you preach if you omit the name of Jesus from your message." (Acts 4:18) However, if we leave the name of Jesus out of our message it won't be a message—it will be only a lecture. We must not turn away from the preciousness of these things. There is no replacement for Jesus' blood. There is no substitution for Jesus' name. Nothing can take the place of His Word. Let's cherish God's presence and cling to Him closely. Let's say, "Lord I don't want to do anything to displease you." Some people say, "What can I get away with and still go to heaven?" That's the wrong attitude. The right attitude is, "Jesus what can I do to please you more?" When my daughter was a little girl, she would come to my wife and/or me at the end of the day and ask, "Do you think I did anything to displease Jesus today?" That is the attitude each of us should have continually in our hearts.

The story in II Samuel 6 ends with the Israelites successfully bringing the Ark to Zion. This teaches us that if we transgress along the way, Jesus will forgive us. He may correct us, but He will receive us back. He's going to stay right beside us. May the presence of Jesus be as precious to us as the Ark was to the children of Israel. They knew that when they went to battle without the Ark, they would be defeated. When they took the Ark with them, they knew they were going to be victorious. Let's live that way — taking Him with us everywhere we go. Let's obediently follow in His way that He might be pleased.

I invite you to pray with me. "Lord, I'm so glad for Your presence. I'm so glad You moved into my life. I want to honor Your presence. I don't want to compromise. I don't want to become familiar to the point of contempt. I don't want to get to the place that I'm so independent that I only go to You when there's no other alternative. I want to talk to You every day. I want to love You and walk with You. I want to grow closer to You. I want to please You in all that I think, say, and do. Amen."

CHAPTER 10

Abandoning the Past for Jesus

I love the gospels. I spent several years studying the principles that have been so carefully recorded by the Holy Spirit during the earthly ministry of Jesus. I wanted to see what He did, how He did it, what He said, and how He said it. My desire is to learn and apply His truths and principles so I can please the Lord with each passing day. The healing of blind Bartimaeus is an event from which we can learn many outstanding principles, including the powerful principle of "abandoning the past for Jesus."

The healing of Bartimaeus took place in the city of Jericho near the end of Jesus' earthly ministry. Jericho was a very wealthy city during that time, so beggars typically would gather at the gate, hoping to receive blessings, and as people passed into and out of the city, they gave alms to the beggars. Day after day, the beggars looked for the handouts that would sustain them and help them to survive another day. Their entire lifestyle was one of begging and seeking to receive. Bartimaeus was one of the beggars at the gate of Jericho.

Mark 10:46-52 declares, "And they came to Jericho; and as he went out of Jericho with his disciples and a great number of people, blind Bartimaeus, the son of Timaeus, sat by the highway side begging. And when he heard that it was Jesus of Nazareth, he began to cry out, and say, Jesus, thou son of David, have mercy on me. And many charged him that he should hold his peace; but he cried the more a great deal, Thou son of David, have mercy on me. And Jesus stood still, and commanded him to be called, And they call the blind man, saying unto him, Be of good comfort, rise; he calleth thee. And he, casting away his garment, rose, and came to Jesus. And Jesus answered and said unto him, What wilt thou that I should do unto thee? The blind man said unto him, Lord that I might receive my sight. And Jesus said unto him, Go thy way, thy faith hath made thee whole. And immediately he received his sight, and followed Jesus in the way."

Of the many miracles Jesus performed, the Holy Spirit selected certain ones to be recorded in Scripture. He impressed it upon the writers to record specific miracles, because those miracles contain principles that we need to learn and apply to our lives today. Therefore, when we study these things, let us not reflect upon them simply as historical accounts, but rather let us open our hearts and ask the Holy Spirit to show us the principles that are vital to our lives.

Son of Timaeus

As Jesus was leaving Jericho, the Holy Spirit suddenly shined the spotlight on one man. There were many people following Jesus. As He walked along, there must have been significant noise from the crowd that followed Him. Perhaps the people would talk to one another, pointing out certain things and discussing what Jesus said and what He was doing. In the midst of what was a large throng of people, the Holy Spirit calls our attention to a man named Bartimaeus, who was a blind beggar.

Bartimaeus is an interesting word. It's a patronymic, which is a word that speaks of his heritage and family. Whenever the prefix "Bar" was placed in front of a name, it meant "the son of, the descendant of, or the seed of." Therefore, "Bartimaeus" literally means "son of Timaeus."

When Jesus stood trial in Pilate's judgment hall, a murderer named Barabbas was brought before the people also. Barabbas stood on one side and Jesus stood on the other. Pilate asked the crowd who they wanted him to release, Jesus or Barabbas. The name "Barabbas" means "son (Bar) of a father (Abba)." On the other side of Pilate stood Jesus, the Son of the Father. Please note the contrast of flesh and spirit between "son of a father" and "Son of the Father."

The Book of Acts introduces a man called Barnabas. The word "Nabas" means "one that comforts, one that exhorts." Barnabas' birth name was Joseph, but he was the son of an exhorter, a comforter, who went about blessing and encouraging people, so people began to call him Barnabas.

When Simon Peter first came to Jesus, He called him by name, "Simon Barjona." What was Jesus saying? He was saying, "You are the son of Jona," (actually Johanan in the Greek language), "But you shall be called Cephas (Peter) which means 'a stone.'" Jesus changed Simon's name to Peter.

One of the twelve apostles was Bartholomew. Matthew, Mark, Luke and Acts all call him "Bartholomew," but John, in his Gospel, calls him "Nathanael." Actually, his name was Nathanael Bartholomew, but the name "Bartholomew" was a patronymic which spoke of the fact that he was the "son of Tolmai." It spoke of his family heritage. He was Bartholomew, son of Tolmai.

Likewise, Bartimaeus means "son of Timaeus." The word "Timaeus" means "the defiled one." Satan is the defiler. Satan tempted Adam, and Adam subsequently fell and became defiled. Adam then took on a sin nature, and passed it down to us. We are descendants of Adam, the defiled one. You can say that we all came from "The Adam's Family." That is our heritage as members of the human family.

A Blind Beggar

Bartimaeus had two problems. First, he was <u>blind</u>, and therefore he could not see Jesus. Likewise, we could not see Jesus when we were dead in trespasses and sins. Because Bartimaeus was blind, he was led around by people. He always went where they wanted to take him because he couldn't see where to go. This is exactly the nature of our condition while we were in sin.

Secondly, Bartimaeus was a <u>beggar</u>. He was living to obtain, not to give. Please see the picture that the Holy Spirit is painting here. We are descendants of the defiled one when we are born into this world. We can't see Jesus, we're influenced by what others say and do, and we are led around by people from day to day. We are born with a self-serving nature that seeks to obtain, grasp, and gain for ourselves, and we never truly know the joy of being a giver until Jesus changes our heart. Like Bartimaeus, until we meet Jesus, we are in a fallen, selfish, grasping, blind, begging condition. But I am so glad that is not the end of the story – Bartimaeus' or ours!

Bartimaeus "sat by the highway side begging." That's what he did every day because that's all he was capable of doing. He was sitting there, sensitive to the noise going on around him. He couldn't see, but he heard the crowd. He wondered what was happening. He asked his friends, who replied, "Jesus of Nazareth is passing this way." Scripture states, "When he heard that Jesus of Nazareth was passing by, he began to cry out, and say, Jesus, thou son of David, have mercy on me."

I am so glad that Jesus came our way. I am glad for that day when we, as blind beggars, descendants of the fallen one, were favored by Jesus. We might think that we found Jesus, but in fact, He found us. He said, "You have not chosen Me, I have chosen you." (John 15:16) We were too blind to see Him, but

He met us where we were and touched our hearts, and by His grace we responded.

The Son of David

The people told Bartimaeus, "It's Jesus of Nazareth." However, when Bartimaeus called to Him, he didn't call Him "Jesus of Nazareth." He didn't simply repeat what he was told. He cried out to Jesus, "Thou Son of David have mercy on me." For the first time, he was crying for mercy instead of money. He tapped into a truth that the others around him apparently did not know. "Jesus of Nazareth" was His name after the flesh, but "Son of David" was a Messianic title. In other words, Bartimaeus was saying, "You are the fulfillment of everything the prophets have promised. You have come to rule and reign on the throne of David. You are the Messiah." In His humanity, Jesus was known as the Son of Man. In His divinity, He was known as the Son of God. In His ministry, He was known as the Son of David with all authority and power, ruling and reigning, coming to set the captive free and raise the dead. Jesus was the prophesied Messiah who had been awaited for hundreds of years.

Crying Out to Jesus

Bartimaeus started shouting. He had to shout for his voice to be heard over the multitude of people. He cried out, "Jesus, Jesus." He knew if things were ever going to change in his life, he was going to have to get the attention of Jesus <u>now</u>. This was his hour, his time—Jesus was coming his way. Bartimaeus was making so much noise crying out that the people around him said, "Be quiet. Don't make so much noise. You're disturbing Jesus." We can *never* disturb Jesus. He *wants* us to cry out to Him in our trouble. Suddenly the voice of the defiled blind beggar transcended the noise of the crowd and reached the ears of Jesus.

Mark 10:49 declares, "Jesus stood still." Do you want to get the attention of God? Recognize Him for who He is and worship Him for who He is. "Jesus thou son of David, have mercy on me." Jesus heard that cry above all the other noise and nonsense. He always hears the cry of the needy one. He always hears the heart that seeks Him in desperation. "Have mercy on me, thou Son of David."

Jesus stopped, turned to one of His disciples, and said, "Go get that man and bring him to me. Just seconds earlier, people were trying to silence Bartimaeus. Now that Jesus heard him and had called for him, the people changed their attitude and said, "Be of good cheer Bartimaeus, He's calling you. He heard you say 'thou Son of David.' He wants you." This is typical of the fickle nature of many people who waver, waffle, and "change their tune" all too often.

The Beggar's Garment

Mark 10:50 states that when Bartimaeus heard that Jesus had asked for him, he cast away his garment. Please picture the scene. Bartimaeus was sitting there wearing his beggar's garment and holding his beggar's cup. He had been there day after day only to receive, but now Jesus was calling him. You can imagine the thrill in his heart as he threw his old beggar's garment aside.

He made an emphatic statement by throwing away his garment. He could have taken it off, folded it neatly, placed it under his arm, and took it with him in the event he may have needed it again. Or, he could have handed it to one of his friends and said, "Hold this for me please. I may need it later." However, Bartimaeus knew that because Jesus called him, a dramatic change was coming in his life and he would never return to what he had been in the past.

He was effectively saying, "*I am abandoning the past for Jesus.* I don't want this garment anymore. I'm done with this lifestyle. I'm not going to live this way any more. I'm casting aside the *past* for the *future*. There is something better ahead than I have ever experienced, so I no longer need this old garment. You will not find me sitting here by the gate any longer because He called my name. You won't find me being led around by people any longer because He called my name. You're not going to see the same man that you looked upon, laughed at, and mocked. I'm getting out of here and I don't want any mementos of the past. I am not coming back!"

The phrase "casting away his garment" conveys a very powerful principle. I believe that is what we must do, in a spiritual sense, when we decide to follow Jesus. Like Bartimaeus, we must say, "I have a new future now. I'm done with my former lifestyle."

Rabboni – My Teacher, My Owner, My Master

Jesus asked him, "What wilt thou that I should do unto thee?" Jesus never asks a question to obtain information, because He already knows everything. Whenever Jesus asks someone a question, He wants them to hear their own heart in their response. When Jesus asked Bartimaeus what he wanted, Bartimaeus answered, "Lord that I might receive my sight."

The word "Lord" is translated from the word *Rabboni*. It's one of only two times that it is found in the entire New Testament. The other time was when Mary was weeping in the garden on resurrection morning. When Jesus asked why she was weeping, she said, "Because they have taken away my Lord and I don't know where they have taken Him." He turned to her and said, "Mary." Then she recognized Him and responded with the word "Rabboni!"

The word *Rabboni* is derived from the root word "Rab" which means "a teacher or a master." People in that day that were teachers or masters were called "Rabs." If they were teachers that had achieved a certain level of recognition, they were called "Rabbis." "Rab" means "<u>a</u> teacher or master." *Rabbi* means "<u>the</u> teacher or master." When the suffix "oni" is added, *Rabboni* means "<u>my</u> Teacher, <u>my</u> Master, or the one I hold in highest esteem." A lot of people called Jesus "Rabbi," but Bartimaeus tapped into a deep truth and recognized Him as more than that. To Bartimaeus, Jesus was not simply "<u>a</u>" teacher, and not simply "<u>the</u>" teacher. To him, Jesus was "<u>my</u>" Teacher, "<u>my</u>" Master. That indicates possession, intimacy, and relationship. Bartimaeus had it right. He saw Jesus as "the One whom I hold in highest esteem. My Master, my Teacher, the One whom I hold higher than anyone else."

A New Lifestyle

Again, Bartimaeus responded by saying, "I want to receive my sight." I believe he was effectively saying, "I want a new lifestyle. I don't want to live in a self-serving manner. I don't want to be a beggar any longer. I want to live to give." This is the new lifestyle, the change of nature, the change of heart, which comes when Jesus is given control of our life. "Master, I believe that I was born to walk, not to be led around by people. I believe that there is a higher and better way to live. I was born to serve others, not to be served (sitting and begging with my little cup)." Bartimaeus wanted the wholeness that he knew only Jesus could give to a descendant of the defiled one, a wholeness that would so dramatically change his lifestyle that he wouldn't think or act any longer like he did in the past.

Jesus said, "Go thy way, thy faith hath made thee whole." He was acknowledging that Bartimaeus had made an important life-changing choice as He said, "You are now whole, so go your way." Bartimaeus responded, "Your way is my way. I want to follow You in Your way." The Bible informs us, "There is a way which seemeth right unto a man but the end thereof are the ways of death." (Proverbs 14:12) Conversely, Jesus said, "I am the Way, the Truth, and the Life." (John 14:6) We experience a more blessed way of living when Jesus turns us from being beggars (trying to attain, achieve, and obtain) to being willing servants and givers. As born-again believers, we "live to give"—to give truth and resources to others, helping them along their way.

Liberty

The sinful nature is self-serving, self-satisfying, and self-seeking. It's centered entirely on self. However, when we give Jesus control of our lives and we become whole in spirit, soul and body, we gain an entirely new outlook and enter into a new lifestyle. We live to serve; we live to give. The Apostle Paul wrote about this in Galatians 5:1, which states, "Stand fast therefore in the liberty wherewith Christ hath made us free, and be not entangled again with the yoke of bondage." I wonder whether we truly understand the word "liberty." Many people typically think of liberty as a license to do their own thing, but that is not liberty. Galatians 5:13 declares, "For brethren, ye have been called unto liberty; only use not liberty for an occasion to the flesh, but by love serve one another." In other words, He sets us free from the desire to live for ourselves such that we live for God and for others. That is true liberty! That is freedom from self-serving bondage!

Bartimaeus received more than natural eyesight. He received a new lifestyle. He threw away his old garment. He didn't have to be led around by people any longer. He no longer had to be a beggar; now he could be a giver. He no longer had to go his way; now he could go God's way. That's liberty!

Abandoning the Past for Jesus

As born again believers, we do not need to be enslaved to our sinful nature any longer. We have been set free. The blood of Jesus Christ has remitted our sins. We must abandon our former lifestyle and decide to follow Jesus. The thing I particularly admire about Bartimaeus is that he made no provision for returning to his former lifestyle. When he threw his garment away, he effectively said, "I'm not coming back. Don't look for me here tomorrow by the gate. Don't look for me begging with a cup in my hand. I'm going out to bless others. Don't look for me in the old places. I'm not living that way any longer. I've found a new way of living."

I truly believe that when we pursue Jesus uncompromisingly, the inclination or temptation to return to the former lifestyle will dissipate. Like Bartimaeus, we must make a determined decision to abandon the past for Jesus!

CHAPTER 11

Remaining Vibrant and Whole

During His earthly ministry, Jesus said, "If you have seen me, you have seen the Father." (John 14:19) He made it clear that one of the primary purposes that God the Father had in sending Jesus, our Lord and Savior, to earth, was to reveal the heart of the Father to us. As we examine Jesus' earthly ministry, we can gain a greater understanding of the Father, His desire for us, His provision to us, and His invitation for us to become all that He has created us to be.

One of the things Jesus revealed was the Father's heart for the lost. Chapter 15 of the Gospel of Luke contains three parables which Jesus spoke to His hearers. The first parable is about a lost sheep and the second is about a lost coin. The third is commonly referred to as the parable of the prodigal son, and is probably the most well known of the three.

In the parable of the prodigal son, the younger son went to his father and requested the portion of goods that belonged to him. The father distributed his two sons' inheritance to them. By custom, the eldest son would receive a double portion of inheritance from his father. Therefore, in this instance, the older son received two-thirds of the father's assets, and the younger son received one third. The younger son took his portion, went to a far country, and wasted it on riotous living. After he had wasted his inheritance, he found himself destitute and unable even to buy food, so he found a job feeding swine. The Bible says that he was so hungry that he desired to eat the swine's food, but he had nothing to eat.

At this point in the story, the Bible uses the phrase, "When he came to himself." (Luke 15:17) Some translations prefer "When he came to his senses." When the son came to the point of proper perspective, he finally saw things as they really were as opposed to the fantasy he had been living. "When he came to himself," he decided that he would humble himself and return to his father. He reasoned, "I would rather live the rest of my life in the presence of my father than to have all of the material goods in the world." The moment when he realized the importance of being in his father's presence was a turning point in his life.

When the son returned home, his father received him with open arms. The father saw him coming from a distance and ran to meet him, signifying that he had already forgiven him. The father turned to his servant and said, "Bring forth the best robe, and put it on him; and put a ring on his hand, and shoes on his feet: And bring hither the fatted calf, and kill it; and let us eat, and be merry. For this my son was dead, and is alive again." (Luke 15:22-24a) Please note the phrase *"alive again."*

Alive Again!

Later, when the elder son saw the celebration and inquired about it, his father repeated the same words to the elder son, who, of course, was still in the family even though he was not in the house. He said "For this my son was dead, and is <u>alive again</u>." The father was excited about the fact that his younger son was <u>alive again</u>. I am so glad that we serve an "again" God. I am so glad that He doesn't just do something or provide something for us on a single occasion, but He leaves the door open for us to receive again and again.

The word "again" comes from the Latin prefix "re," which simply means "again." The word "alive" comes from the Latin word "viv," which is the word from which we get our English word "vivacious," which speaks of someone that is full of life. Therefore, by using the phrase "alive again," the father was effectively saying, "My son has been revived; he has been made 'again alive' or 're-lifed.' There has been a change in Him and He is 'lifed again.'"

Please understand that the father was referring to the spiritual state of his son and not the physical state, for the son had never died physically. Spiritually speaking, he had died because he had been separated from his father and there was no communion or fellowship between them. He did not enjoy what was going on in his father's house, which was a sign of his spiritual death. But the father, who walked in forgiveness, loved his son so much that he wanted him to experience everything that was available.

To be "lifed again" means "to become active again, to flourish again." It means "to come from a state of being depressed, inactive, or ineffective, into a state of being full of joy, happiness, purpose, life, and meaning." This is our Father's will for every one of us. When Jesus told the parable of the prodigal son, He was revealing the heart of Father God, who has always been a God that desired to revive His people. He is a God of revival. He is a God who re-lifes again and again, because He wants us to remain full of life.

God's Heart for Revival

In 785 B.C., God sent a prophetic voice to the world to bring a word about revival. The prophet's name was Hosea, and he spoke a word from the Lord. As recorded in Hosea 6:2, he said, "After two days will he revive us; in the third day he will raise us up, and we shall live in his sight." Students of prophecy will understand the interpretation of the phrase "after two days" in light of II Peter 3:8 which declares, "One day is with the Lord as a thousand years." Therefore, Hosea was prophesying that after two thousand years, God was going to move in a glorious, mighty revival manner; He was going to "re-life" His people. I believe this to be one of the scriptures which confirm that there will be a great revival throughout the world prior to Jesus' Second Coming. We are now in the prophetic "third day," (after two thousand years), and God is going to revive us. He is going to raise us up and we will rejoice in His presence.

I believe when His church leaves this earth, she will not depart dreary, weary, and weak. She will be vivacious. I see the church going out in glory. I see the church affecting the world in a very powerful way. I see people by the thousands coming into the Kingdom of God.

One hundred sixty years after Hosea, God raised up another prophet by the name of Habakkuk. As recorded in Habakkuk 3:2, he said, "O Lord, revive thy work in the midst of the years, in the midst of the years make known; in wrath remember mercy." The heart of God is not only for reviving us as individuals but also reviving His work, the collective church of Jesus Christ.

Scripture says "in the mouth of two or three witnesses shall every word may be established." (Matthew 18:16) One hundred years after Habakkuk, a third prophetic voice arose speaking of revival. Psalm 85:6 declares, "Wilt thou not revive us again; that thy people may rejoice in thee?"

In 1875, a 35 year old man by the name of William McKay wrote what we now refer to as one of the greatest hymns of the church. The lyrics, which are derived from Psalm 85:6, state,

*"Revive us again, fill our hearts with Thy love.
Let each soul be rekindled with fire from above.
Hallelujah, Thine the glory! Hallelujah, amen.
Hallelujah, Thine the glory! Revive us again."*

The Need to be Re-Lifed

We need to be re-lifed periodically. Why? Because one of the characteristics of life, whether it's physical or spiritual, is that it tends to wane. It tends to become less vibrant, less brilliant, less powerful, and less influential. That's a characteristic of life. Occasionally, life needs to be re-lifed. We need to be made alive again.

Most of us who have lived for several decades can say that we are not what we once were physically. I sometimes say, "I'm a walking economy. I'm experiencing recession of the hairline and inflation of the waistline." I have heard it said that there are two ways you can tell when you're getting old. The first is that when you're choosing cereal, you look for the kind that has fiber in it rather than a toy. Secondly, when you bend down to pick up something you dropped, you look around to see if there's something else you can do while you're down there.

"Waning" is not only a characteristic of physical life, but also of spiritual life. We are confronted daily with pressures, stresses, demands, and distractions, which can, over time, deplete our energy, enthusiasm, and vibrancy. I've heard people say, "I wish every day could be Sunday." However, there's a Monday in every week. Very few people say "Thank God it's Monday" because, for most people, Monday is the day in which they return to the things which tend to deplete their reservoir of energy. Over time, we are all susceptible to fall from the place of vibrancy to the place of feeling empty and finding ourselves in need of re-lifing.

Jesus spoke of that potential when He said, "And because iniquity shall abound, the love of many shall wax cold." (Matthew 24:12) Our love for God has a tendency to <u>cool off</u>. The Apostle Paul described the prevailing condition which would exist prior to the coming of the Lord Jesus Christ with the words, "Let no man deceive you by any means; for that day shall not come, except there come a <u>falling away</u> first." (II Thessalonians 2:3) Many of us know people who were once vibrant in their faith and in their love for the Lord, but their vibrancy has waned and, in some cases, has completely vanished. Similarly, Paul wrote to Timothy, "This know also, that in the last days perilous times shall come" (II Timothy 3:1) and that people would have "a form of godliness, but denying the power thereof." (II Timothy 3:5) The word "deny" means "<u>forsake</u>" as opposed to "refuse." It speaks of knowingly leaving something behind that we once had.

Jesus rebuked the church at Ephesus (Revelation 2:4) because they had left their first love. When that occurs, our love grows cold, we fall away from the Lord, and we need to be re-lifed. There is an occasional need for personal re-lifing in our walk with God.

For example, a cell phone is not useful if it is not kept charged. It may look the same on the outside, its sleek design and bright colors still attractive, but it is useless unless it is charged. Its battery has a tendency to wane and must be recharged in order for it to perform as it was designed to perform.

I believe the same is true in our spiritual lives. We each have a critical need to be recharged, "re-lifed." Twelve times, the Psalmist effectively prayed, "Re-life (quicken) me oh God. Breathe on me again." When a cell phone needs recharging, an alert indicator is displayed and the battery icon may start to flash. What are the "low battery" signs we should look for in our spiritual lives?

When I asked the Lord this question, I believe that He led me to the three recorded occasions in which Jesus "re-lifed" (resurrected) people during His earthly ministry. I believe the answer to my question is found by carefully identifying the "re-lifing" principles which are found in each of these three resurrection accounts.

A Sign of Life: Compassion

Chronologically, the first account of Jesus raising someone from the dead is recorded in Luke Chapter 7. This miracle took place near the middle of Jesus' second year of earthly ministry. He was traveling with His disciples to the city of Nain when they encountered a funeral procession. A young man had died and was being carried in a bier (a large wicker basket) toward his burial place.

Luke 7:12 states, "When he <Jesus> came nigh to the gate of the city, behold, there was a dead man carried out, the only son of his mother, and she was a widow; and much people of the city was with her." The fact that the young man was the only son of a widow was significant, because according to the custom of that day, the young man had the responsibility to protect and provide for his widowed mother. As the widow walked slowly in the procession that day, she was mourning the loss of her only son as well as the uncertainty of her future.

Luke 7:13-15 declares, "And when the Lord saw her, he had compassion on her, and said unto her, 'Weep not.' And he came and touched the bier; and they that bare him stood still. And he said, 'Young man, I say unto thee, Arise.' And he that was dead sat up, and began to speak, And he delivered him to his mother."

Jesus raised (re-lifed) the young man out of compassion for the young man's mother.

I believe that this account reveals that when we lose our compassion for the needs of people, it is an indication that we need to be re-lifed. The prevailing sentiment in our world is "Live for yourself. Do what you want to do. Don't worry about anyone else. Let them fend for themselves." This spirit of the world can easily attach itself to us attempting to draw life out of us. When we detect within ourselves a lack of compassion for others, we must immediately ask the Lord to rekindle our compassion.

By definition, there is a significant difference between compassion and pity (sympathy). Pity and sympathy are actions of the soul. They are emotional responses or reactions to a situation. When we look upon someone's unfortunate situation and "feel sorry" for them, that is sympathy. It is good to be sympathetic, but compassion is the spiritual counterpart of sympathy which takes us from feelings to action. True compassion arises out of the spirit, not out of feelings or emotions. Several times, the Word of God declares that Jesus had compassion on people and healed them. Compassion demands action. Compassion demands that the hurting person's need be met.

At a track and field event in Spokane, Washington in 1976, a number of special needs children entered the 100-yard dash, each with the deep desire to win. When the starting gun sounded, they all began to run as fast as they could toward the finish line. Running was very difficult for some of them. One little boy took only a few steps before he tripped. He tumbled several times before coming to a stop on the hard surface. As he lay there crying, other competitors stopped running, turned around, and looked at him. One or two competitors walked back to the boy, linked arms with him, and they walked across the finish line together. What caused them to respond in that manner? Compassion!

That is a great illustration of the difference between sympathy and compassion. Sympathy will cause someone to stop, look, and feel sorry for a fallen one, but compassion will cause someone to link arms with him and walk with him so that he feels like a winner when he crosses the finish line. <u>Compassion</u> is an indication of being spiritually alive.

A Sign of Life: Hunger

The second recorded resurrection by Jesus during His earthly ministry is found in Chapter 5 of the Gospel of Mark. The story is about a young girl, twelve years old, who was the daughter of Jairus, a ruler of the synagogue. When she became gravely ill, Jairus came to Jesus, requesting that He come and lay His hands on her. As they journeyed, Jesus was intercepted by a woman that had been suffering with an infirmity for twelve years. Jesus ministered to her and then continued on to Jairus' house. When they arrived, several people came running from the house and informed Jairus that they were too late because his daughter was already dead. Apparently they had faith in Jesus' ability to heal the sick but were uncertain about the matter of raising the dead.

It was quite a scene when someone died in those days. The body of the deceased was usually kept in his or her home for at least three days. The family would hire mourners who were paid to lament, wail, and mourn all day. And along with the mourners, there were minstrels playing sorrowful music. This was the scene in Jairus' house when Jesus arrived.

Jesus cleared the house of all of the people with the exception of the young girl's parents and three of His disciples (Peter, James and John), all of whom accompanied Jesus into the room where the young girl's body lay. Jesus took the young girl by the hand, said "Arise," and immediately she was re-lifed. Then He revealed an important principle of re-lifing when He commanded that something should be given her to eat. (Mark 5:43) This is significant because hunger is evidence of life and good health. <u>Hunger</u> is the second sign of being spiritually alive.

Typically, when we are not feeling well physically, we lose our appetite. Others can tell that we are feeling better when we regain our hunger. In this dead girl (Jairus' daughter), Jesus saw someone who had lost her hunger. When He re-lifed her, He immediately said to her parents, whose authority the girl was under, "Give her something to eat." Jesus was effectively saying, "Her life had waned and she had lost her hunger. She has now been re-lifed, and her hunger has returned as a sign of life."

One of the evidences that we need spiritually re-lifed is that we lose our hunger for God, His Word, or His presence. In our busy world, we often continue to submit to the demands of our hectic lifestyles until we are exhausted, and sometimes we don't even notice that our hunger for the things of God has waned.

Jesus, the greatest teacher and miracle worker that has ever walked this earth, would sometimes say to His disciples, "Come apart and rest for a while." Even though they were walking in a close relationship with Jesus, they were human and still needed times of rest and re-lifing. Someone once said, "If you don't come apart and rest for a while you'll simply come apart." I believe that many of us have the tendency to keep going until we can't function well anymore, ignoring the need for rest, reflection, and re-lifing. We need to nurture and feed our hunger for Jesus and the Word of God. "Blessed are they that hunger…they shall be filled." (Matthew 5:6)

A Sign of Life: Faith

The third recorded instance in which Jesus re-lifed someone is found in Chapter 11 of the Gospel of John. This miracle occurred near the end of the third year of His earthly ministry, and was one of the last miracles He performed. It is often referred to as the raising of Lazarus from the dead.

Lazarus was a good friend of Jesus. Jesus spent a lot of time in the home of Lazarus, Martha, and Mary, in the town of Bethany. One day as Jesus was ministering in another place, a messenger brought Him the news that His good friend Lazarus was very ill. I believe that those who were with Jesus when He received this news expected Jesus to immediately go to Bethany because of the gravity of the situation. However, Scripture says that He remained where He was for two more days. By the time that Jesus decided to go to Bethany and actually arrived there, Lazarus had been dead for four days and was buried.

It is significant that Martha specifically said that it had been four days since Lazarus' death. (John 11:39) Jewish mysticism taught that for three days after a person's death, their spirit hovered over their body. They believed that the deceased person could come back to life within those three days, but resurrection was impossible from the fourth day forward – that there was no hope – unless there was what they referred to as a Messianic Miracle. I believe that Jesus did not arrive until the fourth day so that it was clear to all of them that He was the long-awaited Messiah.

After four days, Lazarus' body would have begun to decompose and emit an unpleasant odor. The people who gathered around his tomb in Bethany all believed that the situation was irreversible. Jesus walked into the middle of that doubting crowd and commanded, "Lazarus, come forth." The third sign of spiritual life is <u>faith</u>. We must have faith in the power of God to do that which is impossible to man. When we look at a situation and feel that it is hopeless, it is a sign that we need to be re-lifed. We need to believe that "Nothing is impossible with God." (Luke 1:37)

If we are not careful, we can find ourselves slipping into unbelief and doubt similar to the mentality which is prevalent in our world. The Apostle Paul declared (Romans 12:2), "Be not conformed to this world <don't fit into the world's mold> but be ye transformed by the renewing of your mind, that ye may prove what is that good, and acceptable, and perfect, will of God." In the raising of Lazarus, Jesus changed everything that people were convinced was unchangeable.

Revive Us Again!

I believe that, in these days, not only does the church need to be revived, as Habakkuk said, but we as individuals also need revived. If we're not revived individually, how can we be revived collectively? We must be _compassionate_, spiritually _hungry_, and full of _faith_. Revive us God, revive us. We need resuscitated. We need the breath of God to blow on us once again. That's how we "keep on keeping on." That's why we can continue to serve God even when we are in a seemingly impossible situation. Even if we feel death breathing down our neck, we can keep on going because there is a greater breath – the Holy Spirit – who is continually reviving and resuscitating us.

I once heard a story about a little boy who was staying with his grandmother when a terrible storm arose. His grandmother had been told that he was very fearful of things of this nature. As the storm intensified with torrents of rain, flashes of lightning, and claps of thunder, Grandma began to frantically search for little Johnny. She searched all over the house. She looked under the bed, in the closets, and in the basement, but she couldn't find him anywhere. The only place she hadn't looked was the attic. She climbed the stairs as fast as she could, and as she reached the top, she saw Johnny standing with his nose pressed against the window. As the lightning repeatedly flashed and the thunder roared, she heard him say, "Do it again God, do it again."

That's what I say – "Do it again God; do it again to us. Stir us and quicken (re-life) us. Oh God, do it again. When our compassion begins to dissipate, our hunger begins to wane, and our faith is shaken, re-life us again God. Revive us again!"

CHAPTER 12

Satisfying Your Hunger

God loves you. He wants you to have a personal relationship with Him through Jesus, His Son. There is just one thing that separates you from God. That thing is sin. The only way to satisfy the deep hunger for God with which we are all born is to deal with the sin problem in our lives.

The Bible describes sin in many ways. Most simply, sin is our failure to measure up to God's holiness and His righteous standards. We sin by things we do, choices we make, attitudes we show, and thoughts we entertain. We also sin when we fail to do right things. In short, sin is to miss the mark. The Bible affirms our own experience – "there is no one righteous, not even one." (Romans 3:10 NIV) No matter how good we try to be, none of us does right things all the time.

People tend to divide themselves into groups – good people and bad people. But God says that every person who has ever lived is a sinner, and that any sin separates us from God. No matter how we might classify ourselves, this includes you and me. We are all sinners.

"For all have sinned and fall short of the glory of God." Romans 3:23(NIV)
Many people are confused about the way to God. Some think thy will be punished or rewarded according to how good they are. Some think they should make things right in their lives

before they try to come to God. Others find it hard to understand how Jesus could love them when other people don't seem to. But I have great news for you! God DOES love us! More than you can ever imagine! And there is nothing you can do to make Him stop loving you! Yes, our sins demand punishment – the punishment of death and separation from God. But, because of His great love, God sent His only Son Jesus to die for our sins.

"But God demonstrates His own love for us in this: While we were still sinners, Christ died for us." Romans 5:8 (NIV)

For you to come to God you have to get rid of your sin problem. But, in our own strength, none of us can do this! You can't make yourself right with God by being a better person. Only God can rescue us from our sins. He is willing to do this not because of anything you can offer Him, but JUST BECAUSE HE LOVES YOU!

"He saved us, not because of righteous things we had done, but because of His mercy." Titus 3:5 (NIV)

It's God grace that allows you to come to Him – not your efforts to "clean up your life" or work your way to heaven. You can't earn it. It's a free gift.

"For it is by grace you have been saved, through faith – and this not from yourselves, it is the gift of God – not by works, so that no one can boast." Ephesians 2:8-9 (NIV)

For you to come to God, the penalty for your sin must be paid. God's gift to you is His Son Jesus, who paid the debt for you when He died on the cross.

"For the wages of sin is death, but the gift of God is eternal life in Jesus Christ our Lord." Romans 6:23(NIV)

Jesus paid the price for your sin and mine by giving His life on a cross at a place called Calvary, just outside of the city walls of Jerusalem in ancient Israel. God brought Jesus back from the dead. He provided the way for you to have a personal relationship with Him through Jesus. When we realize how deeply our sin grieves the heart of God and how desperately we need a Savior, we are ready to receive God's offer of salvation. To admit we are sinners means turning away from our sin and selfishness and turning to follow Jesus. The Bible word for this is "repentance" – to change our thinking about how grievous sin is so that our thinking is in line with God's. All that's left for you to do is to accept the gift that Jesus is holding out for you right now.

"If you confess with your mouth, 'Jesus is Lord,' and believe in your heart that God raised Him from the dead, you will be saved. For it is with your heart that you believe and are justified, and it is with your mouth that you confess and are saved." Romans 10:9-10 (NIV)

God says that if you believe in His Son, Jesus Christ, you can live forever with Him in glory.

"For God so loved the world that He gave His one and only Son, that whoever believes in Him shall not perish but have eternal life." John 3:16 (NIV)

Are you ready to accept the gift of eternal life that Jesus is offering you right now? Let's review what the commitment involves:

- I acknowledge I am a sinner in need of a Savior – this is to repent or turn away from sin.
- I believe in my heart that God raised Jesus from the dead – this is to trust that Jesus paid the full penalty for my sins.

- I confess Jesus as my Lord and my God — this is to surrender control of my life to Jesus.
- I receive Jesus as my Savior forever — this is to accept that God has done for me and in me what He promised.

If it is your sincere desire to receive Jesus into your heart as your personal Lord and Savior, then talk to God from your heart. Here's a suggested prayer: "Lord Jesus, I know that I am a sinner and I do not deserve eternal life. But, I believe You died and rose from the grave to make me a new creation and to prepare me to dwell in Your presence forever. Jesus, come into my life, take control of my life, forgive my sins and save me. I am now placing my trust in You alone for my salvation and I accept Your free gift of eternal life."

If you have trusted Jesus Christ as your Lord and Savior, you are now on your way to a new way of living! Spend time with Him each day in prayer and personal worship. Live each day out of the supply of "daily bread" that He provides for you. Get involved in a local church and serve with all of your heart. Your hunger for God will be wholly satisfied as you live for Him and know Him more and more. God bless you!

More Inspirational Books from Dr. Leonard Gardner

Eight Principles of Abundant Living

In this inspiring and thought provoking book, Pastor Gardner examines each recorded miracle in the Book of John to uncover spiritual principles of abundant living which can lead you into a lifestyle of deep satisfaction, joy, fulfillment, and true happiness.

The Unfeigned Love of God

The Bible uses the word "unfeigned" to characterize the indescribable love of God. Unfeigned means "genuine, real, pure, not pretentious, and not hypocritical." This powerful book, derived from a series of sermons by Pastor Gardner, will help you understand, accept, and embrace the incredible love God seeks to lavish on you.

Walking Through the High and Hard Places

Life has its ups and downs. The key to a fulfilling life is learning to "walk through" whatever situation or circumstance you encounter, and to emerge victoriously! The spiritual principles you learn in this book will give you the strength to handle any circumstanc

The Work of the Potter's Hands

You are not alive by accident! Isaiah 64:8 declares that God is the potter, and we are the clay. This book examines seven types of Biblical pottery vessels and the process the potter uses to shape and repair vessels. Learn powerful life lessons and know your life is in the hands of a loving God who is forming you through life's experiences so that you "take shape" to fulfill your unique purpose.

It's All in the Blood

This fascinating book draws intriguing and powerful analogies between the incredible design and operation of blood in the human body, and the life-changing spiritual power and provision that is available in the blood of Jesus Christ.

Like the Eagle

Learn how the eagle's lifestyle and attributes can teach you to "soar higher" in your life, as you become like the eagle in areas such as vision, diet, maturity, renewal, commitment, and living an overcoming life.

The Blood Covenant

Blood covenant is a central theme of the entire Bible, and understanding blood covenant will make the Bible come alive to you in brand new ways. Learn the ten steps of blood covenant, the real significance of communion, the names of God and what they mean, and how walking in a true covenant relationship with God can radically change your life.

Liberating Word Ministries

PO Box 380291
Clinton Township, MI 48038
Phone: (586) 216-3668
Fax: (586) 416-4658
lgardner@liberatingword.org

www.liberatingword.org

BREAD THAT SATISFIES

COMING SOON FROM DR. LEONARD GARDNER:

In This Manner (Principles of Prayer)

Hearing God

Chosen to Follow Jesus

Greater Than the Gates

Hindrances to Spiritual Growth

The Planting of the Lord

Contact Dr. Gardner to:
- receive his free monthly newsletter;
- schedule him for a ministry meeting at your church; or
- order his books or other resources.

Liberating Word Ministries

Dr. Leonard Gardner
PO Box 380291
Clinton Township, MI 48038

Phone: (586) 216-3668
Fax: (586) 416-4658
lgardner@liberatingword.org

Made in the USA
Charleston, SC
01 February 2013